LANGUAGE AND LITERACY SERIES

Dorothy S. Strickland, Celia Genishi, and Donna Alvermann SERIES EDITORS

ADVISORY BOARD: RICHARD ALLINGTON, KATHRYN AU,
BERNICE CULLINAN, COLETTE DAIUTE, ANNE HAAS DYSON, CAROLE EDELSKY,
JANET EMIG, SHIRLEY BRICE HEATH, CONNIE JUEL, SUSAN LYTLE, TIMOTHY SHANAHAN

* Volumes with an asterisk following the title are a part of the NCRLL set: Approaches to Language and Literacy
Research, edited by JoBeth Allen and Donna Alvermann.

(Continued)

The Effective Literacy Coach

Using Inquiry to Support Teaching and Learning

ADRIAN RODGERS
EMILY M. RODGERS

Foreword by Gay Su Pinnell

Teachers College, Columbia University
New York and London

Published by Teachers College Press, 1234 Amsterdam Avenue, New York, NY 10027

Library of Congress Cataloging-in-Publication Data

Rodgers, Adrian.
    The effective literacy coach : using inquiry to support teaching and learning / Adrian Rodgers, Emily M. Rodgers ; foreword by Gay Su Pinnell.
    p. cm. — (Language and literacy series)
    Includes bibliographical references and index.
    ISBN 978-0-8077-4801-5 (pbk. : alk. paper)—ISBN 978-0-8077-4802-2 (hardcover : alk. paper)
    1. Reading teachers—In-service training. 2. Language arts (Elementary)—Remedial teaching. I. Rodgers, Emily M. II. Title.
    LB2844.1.R4R63 2007
    428.4071'5—dc22   2007008899

ISBN: 978-0-8077-4801-5 (paper)
ISBN: 978-0-8077-4802-2 (cloth)

Printed on acid-free paper
Manufactured in the United States of America

14 13 12 11 10 09 08 07   8 7 6 5 4 3 2 1

**To Marie Clay,
who challenges us to ask
"What else is possible?"**

Contents

Foreword

When I talk at meetings or conferences, one question I have been asking groups for the past few years is, How many of you would say that you are in the role of literacy coach? The proportion of each group who raise their hands has grown steadily. Of course this is not a scientific survey, yet the chapters of this book document this growing role in education. The idea of a literacy coach is not new. While it has been around for some time, in-class coaching has become much more widespread. Many educators' hopes for rising test scores are pinned on the coach's success.

In the effort to provide more effective reading instruction, districts have been quick to employ an army of literacy coaches, but many have little or no experience in working with adults. Coaches are provided a few days of training or simply left to rely on their own knowledge and experience of teaching and their own judgment. This makes very little sense. Millions of dollars are spent each year on personnel to fill the key role of literacy coach, yet we do not know much about what coaches do, how they can work effectively, and what their contribution to higher achievement might be.

In this volume, Adrian Rodgers and Emily Rodgers address many questions related to literacy coaching and offer important insights into its potential. While acknowledging the role of workshops, graduate-level study, and university partnerships, the authors assert that more is needed. Literacy coaching offers a promising direction and makes a unique contribution, but only if it is effectively implemented. The authors have provided a rich description of what literacy coaches actually do as they work daily with teachers. This text provides valuable information that will help literacy coaching fulfill its promise and avoid landing in the discard pile of educational innovations.

The authors describe coaching as a skilled and complex activity that takes place within a cultural context that has strong impact on a teacher's inclination and ability to reflect on teaching. You will have a view of this complexity through the case studies and conversations that are presented as examples. You will meet

- Debra and Emma, who compare their classrooms and schools and learn how very different school cultures can be
- Arwa, who as a coach adopts a co-learner stance
- Heather, a novice coach who reflects on the role of talk and how it sustains the group of teachers she works with
- Bonnie, a coach who leads a discussion and simultaneously "reflects-in-action" to adjust her coaching style
- Lily, a coach who works on the nature of good questions
- Maggie, who set for herself the goal of observing more and talking less while allowing teachers to collect their own evidence
- Stephanie, who used notes to help her prepare for more powerful debriefing with a teacher she is coaching
- Mary, an experienced coach and chapter coauthor who gives us a detailed picture of the school visit—what the coach does to prepare, set the purpose and focus, support and observe teaching, do side coaching, demonstrate, and use debriefing to create powerful learning

A central premise of *The Effective Literacy Coach: Using Inquiry to Support Teaching and Learning* is the idea that fundamental change in education is possible only through changes in teaching often based on coaching conversations between the teacher and the coach. While change is a focus of this book, the authors direct our attention toward deeper change that helps teachers incorporate inquiry into practice and document their findings. They see coaching not as a generic exercise or a feel-good solution, but as a path to real change and to teaching that can make a difference.

As indicated by the title, talk is foundational to the process of change. The authors recognize the importance of reflection, but they caution that reflecting may not have the power to solve all problems. Each of us is bound by the culture in which we exist. Teachers' reflections need the scaffolding of coaching or colleague visits to make shifts or refinements in their styles. Rodgers and Rodgers claim that the quality of the interaction—the kind of help that is given and when it is offered—has critical implications for success in coaching. They offer specific ideas about the skillful thinking and decision making that successful coaches use. There is, for example, extensive support for coaches in developing the art of asking questions: preparing them, being direct, detailing steps to use in asking them, stating the purpose of asking questions, waiting for responses, and responding to answers.

Throughout this text you will find a personal involvement with teaching. The authors are deeply involved in the world of teaching. Each chapter is soundly grounded in the research literature but goes beyond it to provide many practical examples. The authors speak from their own experiences in solving the problems of practice, achieving collaboration, helping teachers talk together, and talking with coaches about their work. In addition to their extensive work in many different educational venues, they have rooted this work in two professional development initiatives, each of which provides extensive coaching for teachers: (1) Reading Recovery, which provides an intensive initial year and ongoing professional development for teachers who are tutoring first-grade children having extreme difficulty learning to read, and (2) Literacy Collaborative, a comprehensive school development program (K–6) that provides coaching and other support for classroom teachers. Alongside this practical work, the authors have conducted the kind of precise research that allows them to describe what really happens when coaches coach and when both coaches and teachers learn.

—Gay Su Pinnell
The Ohio State University

Literacy coach Mary Fried (right) reviews student data with researchers
Francisco X. Gómez-Bellengé and Susan Ding from the National Data Evaluation Center
(http://www.ndec.us)

Acknowledgments

This book is the summary of our work with teachers and coaches over the past 8 years. We are deeply grateful to Reading Recovery teachers and teacher leaders for their hard work and willingness to share their learning with us. Our school and university colleagues, especially in New Zealand and the United States, have been invaluable in helping us better understand the professional development of teachers.

Our work would not have been possible without the assistance of the "home team." *Über*coaches Rose Mary Estice and Mary Fried helped us to be better coaches through many observations and conversations. Some of our favorite discussions took place at 6:00 a.m. as we drove together with Mary through dark wintry Ohio mornings on our way to work with coaches and teachers in some country schools.

Mary and Carrie Hung also provided us with valuable assistance in writing about literacy studies and interaction between coaches and teachers, and we appreciate their support. At the same time, Debbie Bowman helped us with the mechanics of preparing the manuscript and prodded us when we needed to move forward with our ideas.

The theoretical work of Carol Lyons and Gay Su Pinnell has been invaluable to us in considering coaching in the larger perspective of professional development; and Pat Scharer's enthusiasm, insight, and knowledge about teacher education has buoyed us during difficult times. Our deepest debt of gratitude, of course, goes to Marie Clay on whose work rests much of literacy coaching in the early grades.

Introduction

For the past several years we have been involved in coaching teachers who are obtaining initial or advanced teaching credentials, or participating in on-the-job professional development. We often talk to and work with fellow teacher educators doing the same work, and we occasionally attend sessions at national conferences on coaching. Recently, however, we have seen a rapid growth in interest regarding coaching (Lyons, 2007). We have noticed unofficial coaching strands emerge at the conferences we attend, such as the National Reading Conference (NRC) or the American Educational Research Association (AERA). Most recently, the International Reading Association (IRA) and the National Council of Teachers of English (NCTE) have cosponsored a national clearinghouse for information on coaching (IRA, 2005–2006).

SOME ESSENTIAL QUESTIONS ABOUT COACHING

Many of us who are active in teacher education are pleased to see this trend of increased interest in coaching, but at the same time we are wary that fads in education come and go even more rapidly than in the fashion industry. For this reason, both those who have been interested in literacy coaching for a long time and those who have recently become interested in coaching must ask a number of important questions:

- What do literacy coaches do?
- Why does this recent coaching trend exist?
- How are coaches selected and funded?
- What are the results of coaching on teaching and, most important, on student learning?
- If coaching does make a change in learning, how does the profession prevent it from being the latest discard on the heap of educational fads?

While these are all essential questions, we are the first to admit that we really don't have very many answers, at least not exhaustive and comprehensive ones. Coaching, like many trends in education, is an example of an idea that seems to hold so much promise that it has got ahead of the very necessary research that needs to be done to help answer a number of questions, including the ones we posed above. We would also add that we did not write this book to try to answer all these questions, since this is work that will take multiple teams of researchers many years to begin to address. Instead, we wrote this book to answer only a part of one question—the one regarding what coaches do. Specifically, this book is intended as a conceptual contribution to suggest how coaches might work together with teachers to talk about the work of teaching and coaching.

Although there are many limitations on what we know about coaching and the scope of this book, we are also aware that our readership likely ranges from fellow teacher educators with considerable coaching knowledge to novices. To help get us all on the same page, let's briefly consider some of the questions we posed.

What Do Literacy Coaches Do?

Because much of the recent trend toward implementing a coaching model of professional development has been a ground-up response to the top-down call for increased school accountability, there are perhaps as many understandings of what a *coach* is as there are sites where coaches conduct their work. In the IRA's (2004) recent publication on coaching, they explain,

> There is considerable variability in the job descriptions for . . . coaches. Some coaches are volunteers with no specific training in reading, while others are school district employees with master's degrees and reading specialist certifications. In some schools, tutors who work with students are also called *coaches*. These individuals have a variety of levels of training. . . . At present, there is little consistency in the training, backgrounds, and skills required for such positions, and there is little consistency in the general competence of coaches, in part because there is no agreed upon definitions or standards for these roles. (n.p.)

Although educators really have not defined many of the roles of the coach, the IRA (2004) borrows from Poglinco, Bach, Hovde, Rosenblum, Saunders, and Supovitz (2003) to explain:

Coaching provides ongoing consistent support for the implementation and instruction components. It is nonthreatening and supportive—not evaluative. It gives a sense of how good professional development is. It also affords the opportunity to see it work with students. (p. 42)

Although the IRA provides a spectrum of roles and a range of possible employment circumstances for literacy coaches, this book focuses on one component of what a coach is and does. When we use the term *literacy coach*, we mean a highly qualified individual with at least a master's in reading, some understanding of professional development, and at least a few years of teaching experience. We think of a coach's primary role as working with teachers to construct complex understandings of teaching with the goal of enhancing student learning.

Now that we have provided a sense of what we mean by *literacy coach*, we should also say what we do not mean. We see the literacy coach as being different from, say, a curriculum coordinator who is situated at the district office. Whereas a coordinator's primary responsibility is writing curriculum, aligning it with local and state mandates and supervising the implementation of programs, the literacy coach works on instruction. In the teaching profession, in which an understanding of the importance of equity is essential, we think teachers are likely to undertake only the hardest parts of professional development with peers rather than supervisors. Since teachers need to undertake considerable risk to attain professional growth, in many ways we need to reduce the stakes rather than raise them. For that reason, it is important that the coach be viewed by teachers as a peer.

Why Does This Recent Coaching Trend Exist?

We think that there are several factors that may be supporting the rapid growth of interest in the use of coaches. Each of these factors comes with a promise and a peril. The first factor is offered by the IRA (2004), which suggests that

The rapid proliferation of reading coaches is one of the responses to increased attention to reading achievement and the achievement gap in the United States. . . . Presidents Bill Clinton and George W. Bush and many state governors have spearheaded these initiatives. The Reading Excellence Act of 1998 under Clinton and the Reading First provisions of the No Child Left Behind Act of 2001 under Bush have allotted large amounts of federal dollars for professional development targeting improved reading instruction. (n.p.)

The promise of this legislation is of course that large amounts of money are available to those states willing to accept the terms attached to the funds, and that in turn some of this money can be allocated to literacy coaching. Yet it is the very nature of such an allocation that imperils coaching. One peril is that coaches must work within the parameters attached to funding, which engenders considerable debate. A second peril is that funding of coaches has gotten ahead of the research base that should underlay coaching if we want it to be a quality professional development effort. A third peril is something that we who work in higher education know quite well: seeking grants. One of the things faculty members are expected to do is obtain grants, but we also know those grants are limited in terms of amount and duration. For that reason, faculty members often live from grant to grant, constantly seeking additional funding. In some ways, federal legislation could be considered just another big grant in that it is limited in amount, and the duration is fixed to the length of a particular administration. While this is a system that might work well for federal governments and for faculty members, we would argue that it is not the way to go about funding a quality district professional development initiative that relies on coaches.

The second factor that we think has influenced the growth of interest in literacy coaching is the belief by many that it is simply a really good idea to think carefully about developing high-quality instruction. While curriculum is something that has received quite a bit of attention, instruction has received much less. We would even argue that what coaches do is provide "response-ability," which we define as the ability of the district to respond to calls for quality teaching and enhanced student learning at the classroom level. What we mean by this is that with increased scrutiny on schools regarding student performance, incredible pressure is being brought to bear on schools and teachers under the guise of accountability. This pressure comes from political forces, from the media, and/or from parents. In turn, district-level and school administrators bring pressure on their teachers to be accountable for test results. This is extremely challenging for teachers, who are torn in multiple directions. On the one hand, teachers interested in honing their instruction to provide quality teaching for their students need to spend their time and focus their attention on their classrooms. On the other hand, the needs of administrators tear teachers away from classroom needs and instead require them to refocus their attention on interpreting test scores and explaining both the scores and the teaching approaches being used. What a literacy coach can do in such a setting is free the teacher from administrative responsibilities so that the teacher can focus on classroom teaching. It is the literacy coach who has the ability to respond—or the response-ability—and to interpret for administrators the progress of children in the school and how teachers are responding to student needs. The literacy coach also has the response-ability to interpret communication coming from the administrators to teachers, with a focus on instructional implications. By this, we mean that the literacy coach may learn of funds that are available for the purchase of children's books and then work with teachers to develop a range of quality selections that will support the work the teachers are doing at the school.

The third factor that we think is key in the rapid interest in the work of literacy coaches, and a component of response-ability, is that the literacy coach is the single person in the entire education system who can sit with a teacher or group of teachers and foster and support a discussion and analysis of teaching. At professional development workshops or in university classes, we are left with short-lived discussions of teaching, but it is the literacy coach who can sit in classrooms and watch teachers do their work. While administrators may come and go to conduct annual evaluations of a teacher, it is the literacy coach who can enter a classroom as someone who is not there to conduct summative evaluation, but rather provide formative support to a teacher. Likewise, with expertise in literacy, it is the literacy coach who can interpret what teachers do and why they do it as well as move discussions of teaching from evaluations to conversations. Most important, the literacy coach recognizes that as a student of teaching, he or she is learning with and from teachers rather than teaching teachers.

While literacy coaching might offer the promise of the best teaching, this promise also comes with perils. The first is a personnel issue. Since teaching is an intensely personal act, is it reasonable to believe that all teachers can, should, or would want to be coached? Is it possible to find a coach who can juggle the multiple responsibilities that come with that position? These are difficult issues that must be considered at the local level by those interested in coaching. A second peril comes in the relationship between the coach and building- and district-level administrators. Since the coach is one of the primary individuals on whom the professional development plans of the district rest, it is reasonable to expect that he or she would have considerable contact with principals and coordinators. At the same time, the coach must be seen by teachers as a peer. For this reason, coaches must undertake the difficult work of constantly negotiating their relationship with both administrators and teachers. A third peril comes in assessing whether the coach has made a difference in student learning. While this is an important question to ask, it is extremely difficult to answer, and therefore the position of the literacy coach may always rest on shaky ground.

How Are Coaches Selected and Funded?

Because coaching positions currently have a broad range of descriptions and funding arrangements, there is no single answer to this question. In regard to the selection of coaches, IRA has proposed that reading coaches not only have an in-depth knowledge of reading, assessment, and instruction, but also be excellent teachers, have some experience with professional development, and be sufficiently skilled at presentation that they are able to share their work in public venues such as at district meetings. As the IRA (2004) explains, coaches should be "skilled in leading teacher groups to facilitate reflection and change" and should "master the complexities of observing and modeling in classrooms and providing feedback to teachers" (n.p.).

While these abilities certainly seem necessary for our vision of the literacy coach, it is one thing to state the requirements and quite another thing to find someone who can undertake such a position. One difficulty posed by our suggestion that the coach is a teacher's peer is that a coach would likely be on the same pay scale as a teacher. Indeed, we know of a number of individuals who would be ideally suited for coaching positions who never applied for them because they saw the additional work they would need to undertake as a coach as being unrewarded by additional compensation.

We have also noticed that at many of the conferences we attend, presenters have often remarked anecdotally that many of their coaches have received some training in Reading Recovery (see www.readingrecovery.org). We'll discuss Reading Recovery and its important contribution to coaching later in this book, but suffice it to say that it may be the kind of professional development work undertaken in Reading Recovery that assists teachers in preparing for the work of coaching.

Although coaching positions may initially begin with funding from a grant, we would like to propose that administrators work hard in the early years to write the coaching position into the annual budget. It is essential that in doing this, administrators also consider a budget for the materials that a coach will need and release time for teachers to meet in small groups with the coach. This might look like something that will need to be decided locally, but we would also caution the district against providing coaches with carte blanche. As a part of our work in teacher education we have spent some time in New Zealand and are always impressed by the quality of the work accomplished by teachers and coaches, despite the truly modest amounts provided by the Education Ministry. What is most impressive there is that educators seem to direct resources into professional development, rather than putting them into the latest program available from a publisher—this latter practice is something we often observe in U.S. settings.

In summary, then, we can say that with the exception of private schools, the decision to hire a coach needs to occur at the district level because the work of the coach is part of the larger professional development plans for the district. Depending on the nature of these plans, the district may see a coach as working in one or more than one building. Regardless of the site for coaching, we see coaches as having very sophisticated grade-level knowledge. For that reason, we see a coach as working with a particular grade level of teachers such as K–2 teachers, rather than with all K–12 teachers. We have also found that funding for coaches can be quite short term. One possibility to ensure funding over multiple years is to make sure the coach teaches children about half the day, since in this way the coaching position is funded as a teaching position.

Once the district authorizes the position, an administrator either at the district or at the building level will need to work out many details. One thing the administrator must be wary of is how a teacher is identified to be a part of a coaching cadre. Throughout this book we have stressed that a quality coach does not judge teachers but rather works with them so that all might better understand teaching and learning. Therefore it is essential that teachers who are to be coached not be individuals viewed by administrators as needing remedial teaching work. Likewise, it is essential that individuals who coach for part of the day not be used as personnel who work with struggling teachers for the other part of the day. Districts should avoid hiring coaches based only on years of service or previous administrative backgrounds; instead they must consider many other factors in the hiring of coaches. School districts who insist on hiring coaches who are not highly trained in both content and how to teach that content will obtain only simplistic approaches to coaching—approaches that may not be effective in changing teaching and influencing student learning. While we cannot provide a lot more direction here about how a district might identify potential coaches, we can conclude that the job of the literacy coach is not something that should be offered as extra work for a coordinator or as something to augment the football coach's contract.

What Do Coaches Do and What Are the Results of Coaching on Teaching and, Most Important, on Student Learning?

As we reported above, there is an incredible range of work undertaken by coaches, and their job descriptions range widely. Toll (2004) and Walpole and McKenna (2004) are educators who are among those recently writing about coaching and both their texts include a host of roles that might be undertaken by the literacy coach. The IRA (2004) summarizes the work of the coach, suggesting that it include

- Training of teachers
- Being an adjunct teacher
- Being a go-between for teachers and administrators
- Being a fund-raiser

We see all these roles as important but think that the training of teachers is the most critical. We don't really like the term *training* since it conjures up in our minds an expert coach who speaks and demonstrates to passive learners. While there obviously is some power in the occasional demonstration, we think that the most powerful aspect of work with teachers lies in the personal contact between coach and teacher as each supports the other in learning more about teaching and learning. It is this focus that grounds this book.

Since many forms of professional development are passive, some professional developers are able to focus on only content without regard for participants. In this book, however, we suggest that the coach and teachers are all active learners. Therefore, the coach must consider a number of issues. One issue is whether the teachers want to be coached. We can imagine that a heart surgeon might attend a professional development conference on surgery as a passive participant, but as soon as that heart surgeon is in the midst of an operation, he or she may not want a coach advising that it be done "this way." Thus we must consider what teachers are likely to get out of coaching, their level of receptivity, and the rules of engagement (or the circumstances) under which coaching might occur. A second issue is how to identify teachers to be coached. Since the purpose of coaching is to support building and district professional development initiatives, the teachers who are selected for participation in the coaching cadre should be those whose work can be influenced in such a way that it can begin to address educational goals. For example, one district might have a desire to support the work of beginning K–2 teachers who are in their first 3 years of teaching. Another district might have a desire to more closely support the work of all second-grade teachers so that students failing to meet benchmarks can improve their performance. In these cases the individuals chosen for coaching very much depends on the district's professional development objectives. Likewise, when and how much a coach works with teachers will also depend on district goals in addition to the needs of students, teachers, and the coach.

Not surprisingly, educators are still developing the knowledge base that informs coaching, and therefore what the teachers and coach discuss when they meet and how they talk about it is still something being developed. Educators have begun to address the issue of knowledge base development with some helpful manuals, but considerably more research needs to be undertaken. This will be difficult, since the priorities for the coach vary from site to site. Even more difficult is linking the coaching effort to enhanced student learning. There are simply so many intervening variables in such an equation that only carefully considered research designs will likely be able to inform the field in any persuasive way on the effects of coaching. Sadly, such designs in education are expensive and take time, which means we may have to wait before such evidence appears.

If Coaching Does Make a Change in Learning, How Does the Profession Prevent It from Being the Latest Discard on the Heap of Educational Fads?

We posed the previous questions to help put all readers on the same page and to ground this book in the larger coaching context, but we pose this question to provoke thought and action among readers. Although there is not extensive research on coaching, we think that the concept is one certainly worthy of additional research. But given the history of faddism in education, it's quite likely that coaching could easily end up atop the discarded-ideas pile pretty quickly. This is especially the case if educators adopt the idea that coaching is something funded by federal money such as that of No Child Left Behind, and as soon as that money disappears, coaches will as well. Although top-down reform initiatives in education are important, we think the real power lies in the ground-up response, and it is here that educators at the school, district, and university levels have the opportunity to think and act in a way that supports the careful study and implementation of quality coaching. To do that, we must first think about the implementation of quality coaching and then chronicle the effects of this work on teaching and learning. Teachers, for example, might undertake action research studies that seek to link the connections between coaching, teaching, and learning, and then share their results with fellow staff, at conferences, or in teacher journals. Coaches, for example, might undertake advanced study at the master's or doctoral level, linking the connection between coaching, teaching, and learning in an attempt to build the coaching practitioner knowledge base. Administrators, for example, could work to develop coaching as a form of professional development hardwired to budgets so that coaches do not rely on grants, or they could seek to use the large amounts of data they collect to determine the effects of coaching. Finally, university faculty should harness a range of research methodologies that can be used to answer in a compelling way whether coaching works and if so, how and in what way. Faculty should also develop courses that will be useful for coaches and that will support their efforts.

PLAN FOR THE BOOK

In *The Effective Literacy Coach* we try to offer our initial understandings of what coaches can say to teachers and what they can do with teachers in coaching settings. Our goal is to focus on the coaching conversations that take place between teachers and coaches. We have arrived at these understandings through our work with teachers and our study of coaching. To represent them in this book we have used a number of strategies. In some cases, we offer hypothetical examples to help think about our teaching. In other cases, we offer composite examples: multiple examples of events that took place over the years in our coaching of teaching that we melded into one example. The advantage of creating a composite is that we can offer a number of illustrations in one example. We also have sometimes taken lengthy cases that we have worked on or developed with teachers and offered them here to demonstrate some concepts related to literacy coaching. For these cases, we have received permission from the teachers involved, and we use pseudonyms to protect their identities.

Context is a crucial factor in education, and in the first three chapters of the book we look at the importance of context in a number of different ways. We begin in Chapter 1 by analyzing the challenges to change in education, including the current state of professional development, and consider the potential of the literacy coach as a catalyst for change. In Chapter 2 we propose that the role of the literacy coach is to promote skillful thinking and decision making and to guide collaborative inquiry. In Chapter 3 we consider the role of emotions and the use of groups as a forum for this inquiry.

With the context of coaching work firmly established, we then discuss tasks that might be undertaken by the coach. In Chapter 4 we discuss the use of systematic observation of teaching and the relationship between the interpretive lens of the coach and subsequent analysis of teaching. In Chapter 5 we discuss the usefulness of reflection in teaching and on teaching, and in Chapter 6 we explain how coaches may be able to use reflective work to scaffold learning.

We then look more specifically at particular strategies that might be useful to coaches. For example, in Chapter 7 we suggest different grouping strategies that might be used by the coach and suggest ways in which these grouping strategies can promote change over time. In Chapter 8 we discuss the usefulness of questions by both the coach and the teacher as tools to promote thinking. We focus on the art of the question, how to use questions, and how to develop teacher understanding regarding questions. In Chapter 9 we think about the important work that can be undertaken when a coach works with one teacher in that teacher's classroom. To help focus carefully on this work, we consider what work needs to occur prior to, during, and after the visit.

In Chapter 10 we discuss the new challenges and the new possibilities offered by the recent increase in literacy coaching. We suggest that we can consider both challenges and possibilities in terms of personal contact and administrative infrastructure. By thinking about the importance of our work with individuals who are a part of a larger administrative context such as a school or school district, we can use coaching as a tool that promotes the empowerment of educators.

To conclude this introduction, we want to relate two chance occurrences that motivated us to write this book. One was a lunch with a university faculty member and dear friend who was sitting with us one day talking about her teaching of college students who were teachers by day and master's students by night. She explained to us that she understood in very complex ways theories that explained reading and writing. She knew how to grade papers from her students. Yet she still did not understand how to talk to teachers about their teaching. "What do I say?" she asked. "What can I do?" A second chance event occurred in the photocopier room when we were talking with another colleague. This colleague was a highly respected and veteran full-time teacher. She also held a Ph.D. and taught master's-level methods courses at night. Our colleague explained how she was leading her students in a curriculum-writing exercise. She explained, "I love writing curriculum. It really helps my students understand how to teach." Since we had begun to understand that talking about teaching was not the same as changing teaching, it caused us to wonder how it was that we could help experienced teachers think about their teaching. This book is the product of those thoughts. Our hope is that it will be useful to the reader in thinking about instruction as well as curriculum and in beginning to answer the questions "What do I say?" and "What can I do?"

CHAPTER I

Changing Teaching: The Fundamental Challenge in Education

With the increasing call for what is euphemistically known as school accountability, legislators, educators, administrators, parents, and even business people have all voiced their claims of how education might be reformed. Calls for change range from increased use of charter schools and vouchers to the dismantling of teacher unions, even from legislators who govern in states where teacher unions do not exist. Teachers, we are told, need to be paid less, or more, or both less and more depending on their performance. In classrooms we learn that teachers should use a scientifically based approach to teaching, but we ignore the fact that the random assignment of students to experimental and control groups with teachers trained briefly in an experimental teaching strategy hardly approximates the real-world tasks of teaching that are complicated by multiple factors. Indeed, while it is useful and instructive to adopt experimental research methodologies with relatively small numbers of students and teachers, it is delightfully naive to then infer that such small-scale approaches can inform in a substantive way how teachers adopt teaching strategies that are new to them or different from how they have previously taught.

So long as education stakeholders continue to focus on pouring old wine into new bottles by changing the nature of the school or the compensation for those who work there, we will have passed up one of the most potent tools for supporting child learning. So long as we continue to tinker with how we package the school, we will have ignored the fundamental challenge in education: If teachers can change the way they teach, they can reach in an even more powerful way the children they were reaching earlier, and they may even be able to reach children who did not respond previously. It is only by studying their own teaching that they hone their instruction in such a way to support students who may not have responded to initial teaching approaches. Although educators can think about changing their teaching by working individually or in small groups without additional support, in this book, we focus on the potential of the literacy coach to help bring about change.

In this chapter we discuss what kinds of contexts teachers and coaches might work in and how these contexts might support and constrain the work of the educators. Likewise we review what professional development opportunities currently exist for teachers and what the role of the literacy coach is with regard to the other professional development opportunities.

In the remaining chapters of this book we describe how teachers and a literacy coach can work together for the purpose of accomplishing change in teaching and learning.

THE FUNDAMENTAL CHALLENGE
TO CHANGE IN EDUCATION

The fundamental challenge in education of changing teaching to better support learning is extremely difficult work for a number of reasons. One reason is that there are a number of cultural factors related to the way schools work that do not support teachers in reflecting and acting on their teaching. A second reason is that the professional development provided to teachers does not support self-examination of teaching nor offer a way to act on take self-examination to change teaching. Finally, a third reason is that as educators we rarely have the opportunity to work in collaboration with others on the difficult task of changing our teaching.

In this book we attempt to address these three reasons why changing our teaching is so difficult. In this section we explore the first two reasons: the constraints posed by school culture and the nature of professional development in education.

Negotiating Context: A Challenge for Coaches

Certainly when we think about the settings in which teachers work— from Nantucket to Nome to the Navajo Nation and from Hell's Kitchen to Hebron to Honolulu—there is an astonishing range of students, teachers, and school cultures in which educators do their work. To capture some of the nuances of school culture, we are going to describe two hypothetical communities. In each, there is a school, which is also hypothetical. We have been in many schools like these, our colleagues who are teachers have described working in these schools, and we feel as if we know these school buildings quite well. Finally, we will introduce you to two fictional teachers, Emma and Debra, who work in these schools and who are composites of a number of our colleagues. Emma and Debra are sisters, and they talk to each other in great detail and with careful analysis about the nuances of the school cultures that pervade their professional lives. We take some time to describe the contexts in which Emma and Debra work because we believe the work of literacy coaches is highly context specific.

A Context of Decline: Pine Woods Elementary. Debra is a few years older than Emma and is a veteran second-grade teacher at Pine Woods Elementary in Grassyfield. Grassyfield is a medium-sized city in the northern parts of a Rust Belt state that has fallen on hard times. As a result, school enrollments have been in decline and the district has seen little need to hire new teachers. Indeed, most teachers on Debra's all-White staff have more than 25 years' experience. This is in contrast to the increasing percentage of African American students enrolled in the school district.

In the past 5 years Grassyfield City Schools has come under incredible scrutiny from both the local press and the state department of education. The department of education had developed a number of indicators such as attendance rates, drop-out rates, and standardized-test results to supposedly gauge the quality of the district. When Grassyfield performed poorly for multiple years on these measures, the state threatened a takeover. After the previous superintendent was ousted and a large amount of money was spent on consulting organizations, a new superintendent led the district out of crisis status and into probationary status. The new superintendent promised continued improvement and pledged that in a few years the district would be the flagship district in the state.

A Context of Growth: Flower Valley Elementary. Recently Debra decided to take her spring break vacation and visit her younger sister Emma, who was teaching about an hour's drive away. Debra noticed that Emma's school district was very different from her own. Emma had taught her entire teaching career of 7 years at Flower Valley Elementary and was also a second-grade teacher. In fact, Emma was one of the most experienced teachers in the school. Flower Valley was located in the medium-sized city of Lakeville, whose origins are very different from those of Grassyfield. Until 20 years ago Lakeville had only one stoplight. That changed overnight when the state government decided to take advantage of the large supply of nearby fresh water that could cool a nuclear reactor, which would generate power for the tristate region. The sudden influx of professionals with disposable incomes meant a rapid increase in the service industry and a building boom. Since school funding was based on both property values and corporate taxes, Lakeville quickly grew from a district with two buildings to a multicampus facility with the best-paid teachers in the state. A large shift had taken place in the economic status of the students at the school. A small number of students still came from the rural corners of the district, but they were much poorer than 20 years ago. Large agribusinesses had taken a toll on family-run farms. A much larger group of students were from middle- and upper-middle-income families whose parents worked in the service and supply industries surrounding the power generating plant.

What was interesting to Debra during her visits to Flower Valley Elementary was how different the culture seemed to be from that of her own school. For example, in her district of Grassyfield City Schools, the newly arrived superintendent had directed a large portion of Title I funds to professional development. At Pine Woods Elementary, Debra had worked with fellow second-grade teachers to identify quality children's literature that would work in conjunction with the reading program the central administration was determined to use. One teacher, who was undertaking doctoral study, worked as a kindergarten classroom teacher in the morning, but then served as a literacy coach in the afternoon. Debra found this especially helpful because the literacy coach was able to visit many different classrooms and then report on the power and pitfalls of the new reading program and the power of integrating children's literature into the program.

Debra found that most powerful coaching sessions took place when teachers met together and shared videotapes of their teaching. One thing in particular that Debra took from these sessions was the usefulness of having the literacy coach work in a facilitator role, soliciting observations from all the participants as the teachers looked at their tapes together. Because the literacy coach was also a teacher who had previously taught many of Debra's students, Debra had a genuine interest in working on the same problems. At the same time, Debra unexpectedly learned a few things from the coach. She learned, for example, that she had been coding and scoring running records (Clay, 2002)—an oral reading assessment that she used on a daily basis—in a nonstandard way and that the changes she had introduced to the administration and scoring of the tool probably affected the reliability of the results.

As Debra was sitting in her sister's teacher's lounge before the morning bell, she was surprised to see that most of the teachers seemed to be Emma's age, but most of the administrators seemed to be much older. She learned later that as the district began to explode with growth, many of the midcareer teachers from the old days became administrators. When Debra visited Emma's classroom she was again surprised. Emma had very few students, as a result of the 15-to-1 ratio that governed teaching assignments in the district. Debra was shocked at the books in Emma's room, mostly volumes in a dated basal series. Debra wondered how such a nice school building could have such old resources, but Emma told her that although the district did not meet the "Exemplary" requirements, it did meet all the "Continued Success" requirements.

A Teacher Analysis of School Context. As they drove home to Emma's, Debra and Emma talked about the differences in their classrooms. Since Emma did not have a literacy coach and had never heard of one, Debra took time to explain the new role. Emma explained that their district did not qualify for Title I funds, but Debra told her that she thought that most literacy coaches, at least in some states, were actually not funded by Title I sources (L'Allier, 2005). In fact, Debra thought that the current teacher serving as her literacy coach might be leaving the district, and she was interested in applying for the job. Debra urged Emma to talk about the idea of hiring a literacy coach in her own school district. Since both teachers met some of the requirements for literacy coaches that we described in the Introduction, Debra and Emma wondered if both might be successful literacy coaches (IRA, 2004).

Debra also wanted to find out a little more about Emma's classroom. She knew that students having reading difficulties were pulled out and sent to a reading resource room across the hall. Interestingly, many of these students seemed to be from the more rural parts of the county. "I thought the master's degree you were working on was in reading," Debra said to Emma. "It is, and I defend my thesis next month. You know, I am the only one in my graduate course who completed the eight-course reading sequence and chose to complete a thesis," Emma explained. "But the district likes that we supply special services to kids having difficulty. So we send them to special ed."

"I thought the kids I saw pulled out this morning were going to the reading resource room," Debra said.

"They are, but the district couldn't find a reading specialist so they hired a special ed teacher instead. She just graduated. I think she did a couple of reading courses. And you know, it's mostly farm kids who go over there. It's such a shame poor kids don't get a chance to read at home."

Debra looked at her sister incredulously. "Emma, we didn't have a lot of money when we were growing up, but you know there was no shortage of literacy in our house. What makes you think there is a shortage of literacy in the homes of these kids? They're on a farm! Think about the specialized literacy that those kids must develop that your other students don't have." They talked some more and as they did, Debra also asked why Emma's students looked so much bigger than her own students. "Is it the nuclear reactor?" she joked. Emma explained that if students came to school in kindergarten and could not pass an initial assessment, the kindergarten teachers "strongly encouraged" that the parents keep the child home for an additional year. "We want to work with the students when they are ready," Emma explained.

"Don't you teach them anything?" Debra asked. "I mean, isn't the point of school to teach students things they don't know? We take any student who shows up!"

"Well maybe that's why your district is on academic probation," Emma reasoned.

School Culture: Challenges for Coaches. What is interesting about our fictional case is the illustration of how important context is, and the implications of this context for building and district leadership on the literacy coach's job. To extend our hypothetical case one step further, let's imagine that Debra and Emma were both hired as part-time teachers and part-time literacy coaches in their respective buildings. In their first year on their new jobs, both would certainly face a very different set of challenges. For example, at Pine Woods Elementary, Debra would have to work hard to build on the apparent success of her predecessor. Debra would also be working in a position and a district facing many political pressures. In this high-stakes setting, Debra would need to work hard on her relationship with fellow veteran teachers, walking the tightrope between being collegial with long-serving teacher friends and negotiating her new relationship with them as literacy coach (Bean, 2004b). She would also need to negotiate a new relationship with administrators and address issues related to the all-White teaching staff and the increasing percentage of African American students. In fact, it is likely that previously she had only met curriculum directors and assistant superintendents at socials or district-level professional events. In her new job Debra would likely be sitting at a boardroom table with these individuals, explaining the implications of administrative decision making on her fellow teachers and herself as well as interpreting (and making sense of) data and trends. Understanding standardized-test results, stanines, analyses on multiple measures over time, and disaggregated and aggregated data would surely represent a new skill set for a veteran classroom teacher. So too would the documentation required for the spending of federal Title I funds (Bean, 2004b). In short, Debra would be making sense of data and explaining its significance for her context.

You might be inclined to think that Emma might have it much better. In some ways she has an almost opposite problem. If Emma were hired she would likely need to do a lot of work explaining that the role of the literacy coach is not a remedial one, as if there were a problem that needed to be fixed. She would need to impress upon both her administrators and her fellow teachers that the literacy coach supports teachers as they work toward an analysis of their own teaching and toward changing that teaching to better support student learning. Emma would need to think about issues related to socioeconomic status and would likely have to undertake a thorough examination of her own attitudes regarding students who are referred for additional services. Emma would also need to think about how services can be provided to students in class and what services could be provided. Most important, Emma would need to think about what kinds of teacher preparation her fellow educators bring to the classroom and how she could build on that preparation to create potent learning about teaching.

Current Status of Inservice
Teacher Preparation and the Challenge to Change

In the preceding section, many of the problems and issues that Debra and Emma would have to contend with are functions of school context. Only near the end of a long list of contextual issues did we note that Emma especially would need to think about the nature of the teacher preparation received by teachers she might coach.

In teacher education, when we use the term *teacher preparation*, we tend to think of preservice course work or fieldwork that university students complete as a part of their studies to obtain their initial teaching certificate or license. In this book, however, when we use the phrase *teacher preparation*, we are almost always thinking about the more advanced work that inservice teachers undertake. This work includes teacher workshops, master's-level study, and occasionally doctoral-level study.

When we consider the role of teacher workshops and graduate studies and then describe that as professional development, we must be wary. We should not assume that just because a teacher completed university course work, he or she has changed his or her teaching. Thus, in order to continue our thinking about changing teaching—which we consider a fundamental challenge in education—in this section we describe the role currently fulfilled by professional conferences and university course work and how the literacy coach may be able to fill the gaps between these very different kinds of teacher preparation.

Changing Teaching: The Teacher Workshop. As teachers, much of our professional development took the form of the "sit-'n-get," whereby we attended conferences, read the handouts that were provided, watched a video, and returned to our own classrooms to attempt those techniques that we judged to be viable.

Given our disparaging use of the phrase *sit-'n-get*, the reader may think that we learned nothing from these one-shot professional development workshops, but amazingly we actually learned some very valuable techniques. Adrian, for example, remembers one 2-hour workshop in which the leader provided a helpful sequence of instructional steps aimed at making poetry more accessible to students. The steps were sufficiently generic so that they could work with most poems (e.g., first read the poem aloud and then have students take a guess at its meaning, then read the poem aloud again and have students look for confirmatory phrases and language, then look for difficult words), but they were sufficiently structured so that they really helped make the poem accessible to students and at the same time fostered a reader-response stance (long before that phrase was even known in the teaching circles in which Adrian was teaching). Most important, Adrian was able to take what seemed to him to be an innovation, return to his own class, and use the technique readily with the desired results. Considering the modest amount of time invested and the minimal amount of buy-in required from the constituents, these are quite amazing results.

What is instructive about this example is that it does capture some of the features whereby a one-shot professional development workshop might work. If we stop to think about the circumstances surrounding this example, we can see that the workshop leader chose to focus on something that could be accomplished in one lesson, such as the introduction of a poem new to the students. Additionally, this particular innovation lent itself to description in a series of steps that easily could be replicated and understood by other teachers regardless of experience level. Finally, it was an innovation targeted at a genre of literature that many teachers find difficult to teach, which ensured a motivated audience likely to attempt the initiative. In other words, the audience bought into the workshop, and there was no need for additional supports from other partners such as the school district.

There is one other instructive feature about this example that has considerable implications for our work as literacy coaches, and that is that in the poetry workshop example, we really do not know how many teachers returned to their classrooms and never tried the innovation. We also do not know how many teachers returned to their classrooms to try the innovation once, have it fail, and then abandon it. And we do not know how many teachers tried the innovation, really worked at honing their teaching to arrive at quality implementation, still failed, and then abandoned the initiative. Indeed we are left only with the one case that we know of, whereby the innovation was described, attempted, and instituted with relative success relatively easily.

Yet this is frequently very similar to how we who write about teaching describe innovation in teaching. Generally in our discipline when discussing professional development, we describe it and represent it as a series of steps; we suggest to teachers that it can be easily done in a 35-, 45-, or 60-minute time period or even a period punctuated by two ringing bells; and we find the case that represents a success, ignoring the multiple cases out there that may represent failure of the initiative. At the same time we know that systemic professional development with a goal of change goes far beyond the one-shot workshop. We are hard pressed to describe what systemic professional development looks like, how it works, and how to describe the outcomes. Additionally, since we feel pressured to show that professional development works, we tend to feature the what-worked component rather than the what-did-not-work, all the while knowing that the most instructive case for us as educators is knowing what happened when things did not work or they went awry (Wilson & Daviss, 1994).

Changing Teaching: The Master's Degree. Teachers who undertake master's-level studies have few opportunities to study their own teaching. The few pedagogy courses that do exist are often limited to one semester, which means that the teachers enrolled have little time to attempt techniques and refine them. Many master's-level students do complete an exit project such as a thesis or portfolio where they can undertake inquiry into their own teaching; however, even with an exit project there are limitations on the power that can be achieved. At smaller institutions, exit projects are sometimes supervised by faculty who are not experts in the area being taught, and therefore these faculty can offer only general advice on the design of the project. Additionally, when master's-level students undertake inquiry into their own teaching, they often do so in isolation, supported by occasional meetings in a graduate-level course and with their faculty advisor.

Changing Teaching: The Doctoral Degree. Even for teachers engaged in doctoral-level study, the scenario for conducting inquiry into teaching and professional development is not much better. Certainly doctoral-level students do have advantages over master's-level students when studying professional development. One advantage is that they have the opportunity to read and study the various literature bases that inform professional development. These literature bases include literature related to the craft of teaching; research that has been conducted regarding certain teaching strategies or approaches; assessments and evaluations that might be used

to either gauge the success of a teaching method or chronicle what occurred; and the burgeoning literature bases related to coaching, professional development, and reform (Wang & Odell, 2002).

In addition to a good sense of the literature that supports professional
development work, doctoral students have the opportunity to sometimes
work as graduate assistants on professional development initiatives affil-
iated with the university. It is here that they can develop a firsthand sense
of the need for buy-in from all partners in the professional development
initiative, including the college of education, university faculty, district-
level employees, school administrators, and teachers (Rodgers & Keil,
in press). Additionally, some professional development initiatives may
have an even wider partnership base, including government-, corporate-,
community-, and family-level supports. The savvy doctoral student soon
realizes that working with such a range of partners requires more than
buy-in; it requires the ability for multidirectional and multilevel communication between partners. By that, we mean that all the partners in a
professional development initiative need to be able to have communication with each other and with other components of the partnership. Additionally, each partner must be able to communicate at different levels.
For example, while the dean of education communicates with the superintendent, the faculty might be communicating with the teachers, and the
teachers with the parents.

Doctoral students also have an advantage over their master's-level
counterparts: They can undertake more complex inquiry into professional
development. One reason is that doctoral students have more complex
supports working on their behalf, especially if they are able to nest their
dissertation studies in a larger, ongoing partnership. Moreover, doctoral
students typically have more time to undertake their inquiry and have the
ability to identify a site that they think will work well in helping them answer their research questions. Despite these apparent advantages, doctoral students also have a disadvantage in conducting their professional development activities, which is that unless they are also teaching in a school
as they complete their doctoral work, they are really working as guests
in someone else's classroom (A. Rodgers, 2002). As a result, regardless of
how well they try to understand the challenges of teaching and working
at the school, at the end of each day they are still able to walk away knowing that their inquiry will soon be complete. The teacher in a particular
classroom, however, has been with the students before the researcher appeared, will be with the students after the researcher disappears, and may
likely be teaching in the school long after the doctoral student has graduated and moved on to a faculty position. This must cause us to question
the veracity of findings from doctoral dissertations in which the doctoral

student can parachute in and out, leaving the teacher behind to deal with the aftermath of innovation.

Thus we can conclude that master's- and doctoral-level studies do have something to contribute to professional development, but that these contributions are constrained by the nature of graduate-level programs. At the master's level, students may have the option to undertake inquiry into their own classrooms, but they sometimes do so in isolation and without daily interaction with others who might be able to assist the inquiry. On the other hand, at the doctoral level, students have the opportunity to be a part of larger initiatives related to systemic reform. When it comes to gathering classroom-based data to document the reform initiative, however, doctoral students are at a disadvantage in understanding how reforms are working at the classroom level because of their outsider status.

The Role of Faculty in Working with Teachers. Like doctoral students, university faculty involved with reform initiatives face many of the same limitations and actually some additional ones as well. Because they are typically employed full-time at the university, teachers may actually view some faculty as having even more of an outsider status than doctoral students. At the same time, university faculty have many responsibilities to meet. These responsibilities can include the need to teach on campus in addition to undertaking fieldwork; the need to find funding that supports professional development initiatives; the need to meet human-subject review requirements that may limit the scope of classroom-based professional development initiatives in order to protect participants against perceived risks; and the need to collect, analyze, and report in blind, peer-reviewed journals the findings of the professional development work.

We can conclude from this review of the roles of teachers, students, and faculty that undertaking professional development work is difficult because of systemic constraints imposed on us by the nature of our work. It is no wonder, then, that professional development initiatives are often limited and fleeting in their length or scope. It should not come as a surprise that in many settings, the one-shot workshop continues to be the primary form of professional development for teachers and that frequently, teachers find it frustrating to work with professional development initiatives, whereby well-meaning individuals with some expertise parachute in to share some insight or program, leaving teachers to make sense of how that insight or program is to work in their classroom after the individual leaves.

LEVERAGING THE ROLE
OF THE LITERACY COACH AS A TOOL FOR CHANGE

As long as educators rely on teacher workshops, graduate-level study, or partnerships with colleges of education to address educational reform, we will be hard pressed to address how we can make teaching children even more potent. Since workshops and university course work entail a limitation imposed by the system, what we can do is try to develop roles in the educational system that can help us fill the gaps left between the various types of professional development offered to teachers. One of these roles is the development of the literacy coach. Certainly the concept of a coach for teachers has been around for a number of years, but it has gained renewed interest recently for a number of reasons, including the publication of books that discuss the role of the literacy coach (Bean, 2004a; Lyons & Pinnell, 2001; Lyons, Pinnell, & DeFord, 1993; Toll, 2004; Walpole & McKenna, 2004), the availability of funds to support literacy coach positions (L'Allier, 2005), the articulation of guidelines regarding coaching from learned societies (IRA, 2004), and the pressure for schools and school districts to be accountable for the results of children on standardized tests.

Flexibility and the Literacy Coach

One of the interesting features of the literacy coach's role is considerable flexibility in how coaches are employed in the educational system, how they are funded, and what they do (Toll, 2005). Although this flexibility sometimes makes it hard to describe what literacy coaches do, there is considerable strength in flexibility, since it means that each coach can articulate his or her position in addressing the gaps that occur between other professional development initiatives in a school or district. Although literacy coaches are used in different ways by different schools and school districts, they do tend to be accredited as teachers and employed either by the school or district. This is an important feature. Depending on how a school district has decided to use literacy coaches, certainly there is the possibility that literacy coaches will be viewed as fellow teachers who can work with both students and teachers in classrooms. Most important, as fellow teachers literacy coaches understand the culture and history of the school and the district, and their involvement in the school or district can be seen as much more long term than that of outside consultants. Like teachers, literacy coaches have a stake in children's performance on standardized tests and therefore in honing instruction to meet student needs.

Fostering Dialogue: Coaching Conversation

Although a part of coaching teachers is observing and sometimes modeling lessons, what is most essential is fostering dialogue or *coaching conversations* about teaching. By supporting and fostering conversations about teaching, both between the teacher and the coach and among teachers and other teachers, the coach has the opportunity to provoke not only deep reflection but also action regarding teaching. Through careful analyses, teachers have the opportunity to enhance practices that work, reform practices that don't work as well as they could, and abandon practices that seem to hinder what works. Most important, the teacher can arrive at these decisions through collaboration with others in a supportive setting. It is this kind of collaboration that is potent enough to provoke teachers to actually change their teaching practices because they have decided they need to and not because someone else told them to. As we all know, deciding to change a particular routine is one thing, but actually doing it is quite another. This is because our teaching performances are quite complex, and they hinge on a number of factors. Thus the literacy coach can assist reform-minded teachers by giving feedback about what the teacher is trying to change. The literacy coach can observe teaching sessions, review student work, and debrief lessons with the teacher; this enables the teacher to determine how he or she is progressing in the changes that need to be made in the teaching.

Literacy Coach: Expert Teaching or Teaching Expert?

What we like most about the concept of the literacy coach is that a coach recognizes and values the expert role of the teacher. If we think about other professions in which coaches are involved, such as in professional sports, acting, or singing, no one doubts that it is Tiger Woods or Michelle Pfeiffer or Luciano Pavarotti who are the experts in their field. The golf, acting, and singing coaches of these eminent professionals may indeed be expert in their own right as golfers, actors, and singers, but this is not what they're known for. What the coaches are known for is their ability to *teach* golf, acting, and singing. Likewise, while a literacy coach is an expert teacher, coaches are selected because of their ability to teach teachers in an expert way. And that teaching of teachers is by no means done exclusively through direct instruction. Instead, it is the role of coaches to support the professionals in doing what the latter can do best by supporting study and analysis of the activity, thereby freeing the professionals to create their best performance. Likewise, literacy coaches do not dictate to teachers what to do, but rather observe, analyze, and discuss in pairs and groups to support the work of teachers. It is in this coaching role that literacy coaches can achieve their most powerful opportunities to foster *response-ability*. In the Introduction, we define response-ability as the district's ability to respond to calls for quality teaching and enhanced student learning at the classroom level. By helping teachers change their teaching practices one professional at a time, coaches ratchet up the ability of an entire school to respond to the needs of students.

Over the years, we have worked in many coaching settings with preservice and inservice teachers. In these settings we have been very interested in how we gather information regarding teaching, how we conference with teachers about what we have observed, and how we can help them hone their instruction so they can achieve in an optimal way what they set out to achieve. In thinking about this work, we realize that we are by no means experts. In fact, we realize that this book is the beginning of our understanding of coaching rather than the end of it.

SUMMARY AND NEXT STEPS

We began this chapter by setting the context of the perceived increasing pressure on public schools to improve results on standardized tests or measures of performance. We proposed that professional development workshops and university course work was one way to do this, but that the opportunity to study one's own teaching for the purpose of creating even more powerful student learning remains very much hit or miss. We conclude that the role of the literacy coach is one that supports conversation about teaching, and in the current educational culture it is necessary to support teachers in thinking about their teaching.

It is our hope that you will join us as we begin our journey toward learning more about literacy coaching, what we can do as we coach teachers, and how we can talk about it together. In the following chapter we begin our journey by considering how coaches can guide inquiry. This concept of guiding suggests a twist on the old adage that writers must "show, not tell." As we will learn, literacy coaches must "tell, but only sometimes; guide, at other times."

CHAPTER 2

The Role of the Literacy Coach: Guiding Inquiry for Literacy Learning

Michael Fullan (1993) famously noted in *Change Forces* that change cannot be mandated, not when the nature of change requires skillful thinking and decision making. Fullan was referring to large-scale educational reform, but the same is probably true about coaching change at the day-to-day level of instruction. In Fullan's reasoning, simple changes such as using new, updated forms or revising the dates for ongoing monitoring of student progress probably can be mandated without too much trouble, but changes to how and what we teach are much more complex and likely to fail if simply mandated.

What does a coaching mandate for instructional change sound like? We heard recently from a district administrator who was lamenting the way teachers in the district were being coached. The teachers were taking on a new literacy program that required them to teach and respond to children in substantially new ways; however, when they pressed their literacy coach for rationales, they were told, "You have to do it this way because that's what the program says. Don't question it." Of course, the district administrator advised the teachers to keep on asking questions. He understood that making teaching decisions in the moment requires skillful thinking and deep understanding of rationales, and that the coach's approach to simply mandate change was not likely to bring about the needed fundamental change to instruction.

Pinnell and Rodgers (2002) describe coaching decisions as existing along a continuum of support from directed application on one end, where the coach provides specific, direct information, to open application on the opposite end, in which the coach provides a forum for examining principles of instruction, suggests materials to use, and works with the teacher to develop alternative teaching moves. Along the continuum the coach's support shifts from being less directive to being more of a collaborator in the inquiry process. A coach can move along this continuum of support within a single coaching session, providing explicit direction when direct instruction is appropriate and supporting a forum for inquiry when more skillful decision making is required. Conceptualizing coaching decisions as existing along a continuum suggests that there may be times when the coach has to mandate change and other times when the coach's role is to provide a forum for inquiry.

In this chapter we explore that further end of the decision-making continuum: the coach's role in providing a forum for inquiry. We assume that it is easy for coaches to decide when it's appropriate to mandate change ("Use these new forms from now on." "Take a running record every day"). Not so easy, though, is deciding when and how to support teacher inquiry.

We begin by describing the coach's role and then discuss how the coach can use collaborative inquiry to support teacher learning. Along the way we draw from our case studies of coaches guiding inquiry in order to articulate principles of effective coaching conversations.

PRIMARY ROLES OF THE COACH

According to the International Reading Association's (IRA's) 2004 statement on coaching, reading coaches must be excellent teachers; have in-depth knowledge of the reading process, assessment, and instruction; have experience working with teachers; and be excellent presenters. The IRA (2004) statement also draws heavily from Rita Bean's (2004a) description of the work of coaches. Bean described three levels of coaching activities, ranging in intensity from least to most. Some of the least intense activities involve developing relationships with colleagues, helping to locate and provide materials, and helping with student assessment. These activities are perhaps the least intense because they simply involve being a knowledgeable, supportive other—someone who can provide support in getting the work done. In these cases, the coach can be perceived almost as an extra pair of hands. The most intense coaching activities, according to Bean, include modeling, co-teaching lessons, providing feedback to teachers, and analyzing videotaped lessons of teachers.

While effective reading coaches do need to be organized, good communicators, and able to manage notes and schedules, we think their primary role is to scaffold teacher learning and support reflection. This aspect of the coach's role resides in the most intense kind of activity that Bean describes and is the focus of the remainder of this chapter.

COACHING SKILLFUL THINKING AND DECISION MAKING

Coaches, we are told, are "respectful of others' knowledge," "good listeners," and "passionate and empathetic" (National Council of Teachers of English [NCTE], 2004, p. 1). These characteristics are echoed in the responses of literacy coaches who were asked, "What makes an effective reading coach?" (Dole, 2004). The coaches surveyed in Dole's study said that effective coaches need to be reflective, to be able to "support and nudge," and have a good sense of humor (p. 469).

Effective coaches, it seems, take on a co-learner stance. By this we mean the coach learns about teaching with teachers rather than being a person who claims to "know and tell" teachers what to do. To help the coach learn about teaching, the coach supports the self-reflection and self–analysis of both coach and teachers, but the coach does not evaluate as administrators would (Strickland, 2004). This co-learner stance includes the goal of providing teachers with feedback on their teaching (the central feature of the coach's role, according to IRA, 2004), but goes beyond it to support and nudge reflection and self-analysis.

We know that teachers are highly reflective and that there is an extensive literature base on this. Because teachers are so reflective, coaches can't simply say, "Do it this way because that's the way the program says to do it." That approach might change teaching for as long as the coach is present, but the change is unlikely to endure longer than that. As soon as the coach leaves and the door is closed, the teacher will likely return to old ways of teaching. In addition, the teacher is likely and understandably going to hold a poor view of the coach.

This makes sense: As long as the coach works at a surface level, the teacher will not work toward change. Instead, the coach must understand why teachers make the instructional choices that they do, pose rationales for other instructional possibilities, and work together toward change.

To understand how coaches coach skillful thinking and decision making, we should first understand how learning occurs and the role that language and language interactions play in the learning process. We examine these next and then consider how coaches provide a forum to support collaborative inquiry.

Using the Knowledge Base to Coach: Learning and the Role of Language

We use a sociocultural lens to understand learning. From this perspective, there is no time out from one's culture. Learners are actively participating with more knowledgeable others in their cultural practices (Rogoff, 1997). By this, Rogoff means that initially the learner requires assistance from more capable others, but gradually, as capacity develops, participation becomes more self-regulated and independent. Learning can be defined, then, as change in the way a learner participates in activities over time. This changing participation is just what Vygotsky (1978) was describing in his conceptualization of cognitive development as progress through a zone of proximal development. In concrete terms, we know that learning has occurred when we see changes in how we are able to participate in an activity such as learning to ski, drive a car, ride a bike, or read a book. Where help was once needed, the learner can now participate independently without guidance. The change in participation—or the learning—comes about as a result of social interaction with more knowledgeable others.

Rogoff (1997) wrote about teaching and learning in much the same way, describing the process as guided participation in an activity; Tharp and Gallimore (1988) referred to it as assisted performance. Both expand on Vygotsky's (1978) original description of the nature of cognitive development. The central features of this view of learning include the significant role of interacting with others, the social nature of learning, and the important notion of changing participation in an activity as evidence of learning. The coach's goal, therefore, is to support the way teachers teach so that a teacher is able to work with increasing flexibility and independence from the coach's help. Evidence of learning comes in the form of the teacher's doing things differently.

Think about this view of learning as you consider a coach's response to Emily's question, "How do you know if your coaching has made a difference?" The coach replies, "If the teacher is enthusiastic about the changes that I've suggested and not resistant to the ideas, then I know I've made a difference." Maybe. Feeling good about a coaching interaction or warmly receiving a coach's suggestion is a good sign, as we will discuss in Chapter 3 when we describe the affective dimension of learning, but just being receptive and enthusiastic about change is not enough. According to our Vygotskian definition of learning, we should look for changing participation in activities as evidence of learning. Where once the teacher needed the support of a coach to guide discussion groups, for example, the teacher can now work independently and flexibly without the coach's support.

Rogoff (1990) also described learning as changing participation in an activity, but she added the important role of guidance in the process. The more knowledgeable coach guides the learner's participation in the activity by arranging for the learner to assume an increasingly independent role.

The collaborative processes of guidance and participation are essential, she said, to build bridges from present understandings to new ones. Rogoff's view places a special emphasis on the role of the coach, who is charged with arranging experiences in such a way that the learner, or teacher, can participate with more independence.

Language is a critical tool in this change in the learner's way of thinking and responding because it becomes an instrument for planning and carrying out action—a way to sort out one's thoughts (Luria, 1982). This emphasis on language as a tool for learning is supported by the theoretical works of Vygotsky and Luria (see, e.g., Luria, 1979, 1982; Vygotsky, 1978). In fact, as Wells (2000) has noted, there is complete agreement about one feature of the zone of proximal development: the central role of language in learning (p. 57).

Articulating the Work of Coaching

Humans make progress in leaps and bounds in large part because of our ability to use language and to share and build on the ideas of others. As Michael Halliday said, "Language is the essential condition of knowing, the process by which experience becomes knowledge" (quoted in Wells, 2000, p. 73). It allows for people to build knowledge together and provides the context for learning (Wells, 1999). As such, Wells noted, learners need to be able to express their opinions and comment on and question other people's beliefs in order for the group to develop new understandings.

The challenge of guiding inquiry in this way is captured in the following reflection from Bonnie, a literacy coach:

> I listened to audiotapes of my coaching and realized that I was doing a lot of telling instead of providing opportunities for teachers to discuss issues. I was unaware of the level of my control until I heard myself on the tapes. I decided to focus on being aware of what I was doing before I blurted out things that took away from the teachers' participation. I have made some progress in this area. I'm more aware of when I'm about to respond, and then make myself pause for a couple of seconds to think about the best approach to get teachers involved. Even without audiotaping my coaching I know that I am doing a better job of not just telling but fostering teacher participation in the discussion instead.

Another literacy coach, Lily, reflected recently on the challenge of asking questions that foster discussion rather than simple agreement with the coach. She wrote:

Questions that can be answered with a simple yes or no are the kinds of questions that signal to the teacher that the coach has only one acceptable answer in mind. Rather than trying to come up with questions on the spot after observing a teacher, I write them while I'm observing. This gives me more time to think about how to frame questions that will foster discussion.

It is evident from Bonnie's and Lily's reflections on their coaching that providing a forum for inquiry is tough work. Even when the coach is well intentioned and focused on fostering discussion, the dialogue between coach and teacher can become didactic, with the coach doing most of the talking. Our understanding of learning and the central role of language in shifting participation in activities underscores the importance of discussion and dialogue, yet our experience demonstrates how challenging it is to guide inquiry around skillful teaching and decision making.

In the section that follows we draw from Lindfors's (1999) work on collaborative inquiry to articulate principles of effective coaching conversations to foster discussion and new learning, not simply to obtain agreement with the coach's views. Lindfors's conceptualization of language interactions as collaborative inquiry provides some guidance on how language acts might support learning.

Conceptualizing Collaborative Inquiry: A Forum for Coaching Skillful Thinking

Lindfors (1999) defines *inquiry* as *"a language act in which one attempts to elicit another's help in going beyond his or her present understanding"* (p. ix, italics in original). We can't think of a better way to describe the goal of talking about teaching: to help one another go beyond present understandings to new insights. Lindfors had groups of students in a classroom in mind when she described principles of collaborative inquiry, but they apply equally to coaching teachers. In our coaching work, we use these particular principles from Lindfors's work to establish a forum for discussion and inquiry in coaching settings:

- Inquiry's stance is uncertain and invitational. This means that all participants, including the coach, can be genuinely perplexed, wonder about things, and ask questions to which they don't know the answer. (p. 124)
- Questions can be posed by the coach or the teachers, and they are regarded as invitations to inquire. Others must accept the invitation,

even if it means putting aside their own questions for the moment. (p. 124)
- Acts of inquiry should be handled with care. It's easy to offend. (p. 194)

We describe these principles for collaboration to teachers with whom we work right from the outset of our coaching. We didn't always do it this way; we used to simply keep them in mind as we worked together with teachers. We soon realized, however, that explicitly sharing the expectations for our inquiry together meant that we could develop a more collaborative relationship that much faster. In other words, knowing their roles and responsibilities in these acts of inquiry from the start allowed teachers to establish a supportive forum for discussion sooner.

Lindfors (1999) also described how she thought collaborative inquiry might be carried out in classrooms. Again, in our coaching experience, we have found these guidelines from Lindfors helpful in supporting our inquiry:

- Exploring, not answering, is central to the process.
- Paraphrasing remains true to the speaker's intent.
- Listening to others and building on responses is necessary.
- Keeping the inquiry going is the key. (p. 208)

Similar suggestions for coaching have been advanced elsewhere. Lyons et al. wrote in 1993 about the important role of language in coaching instructional change. They described the nature of interactions in coaching, drawing from the work of Michael Halliday, who wrote about language learning as learning how to mean (see, e.g., Halliday, 1975). In their volume *Partners in Learning*, Lyons, Pinnell, and DeFord (1993) identified six principles for guiding inquiry in a coaching setting: (1) using a constructivist view of learning, (2) using language to learn, (3) valuing tentativeness, (4) maintaining flexibility, (5) creating supportive networks for learning, and (6) maintaining ongoing learning.

Lyons and her colleagues emphasized principles for using language to guide collaborative inquiry in a coaching context similar to those Lindfors (1999) described for teachers working with students in classrooms. The overlap is not surprising. In both settings learners are guided to inquire together to reach a deeper level of understanding than they could achieve individually. We turn now to examples from our experience coaching coaches in order to explore these principles of guiding collaborative inquiry within a coaching setting.

Guiding Collaborative Inquiry: Learning from Coaches

In the examples that follow, the coach has just observed the teacher giving a literacy lesson and is now debriefing with the teacher. We purposefully selected examples in which a coach is working with one teacher who is teaching one student because we wanted to keep a sharp focus on the nature of the coaching. There is another layer of professional development in this case, however, in that the coach, Heather, is also being coached, in this case by Emily. After the coaching session, Emily and Heather will debrief about how things went and set new goals for coaching a second teacher. As you read through the transcript of Heather coaching the teacher,

- Reflect on the principles of guiding inquiry that we just described.
- Think about what shift in teaching or understanding Heather is working toward with the teacher. Did she lift the teacher's understanding?
- Decide what feedback you would give Heather on how she guided the inquiry, if you were coaching her.

A Coaching Session. The following is an excerpt of a teaching session between Heather and a teacher.

> HEATHER: How would you describe the student's fluency when she read the first story?
> TEACHER: It was choppy and word by word. She was checking each word carefully as she read.
> HEATHER: Yes, it was choppy. You used the two masking cards to show her phrases in the text so she could group those words together and sound more phrased. Let's look in Clay's (1993) guidebook to see the purpose of teaching students to read in a phrased and fluent way. [Coach reads aloud from the guidebook, then continues] So we want her to read in phrases. She was choppy right here [pointing to a text that the child had read] when she read, "Gaby . . . was . . . hungry." [Coach uses two cards to show two phrases: *Gaby/was hungry*. Teacher looking away and writing notes during this demonstration.] So, I'd like to see her read in a more phrased way. Right now she looks at the pictures for too long, and she's choppy when she reads.

TEACHER: So you're saying I should be quiet while she's rereading a familiar book?
HEATHER: What do you think?
TEACHER: I could just let her go ahead and read and see what she does on her own.

The imbalance of turn taking is quite obvious when you read a transcript of the coaching, but it was just as apparent hearing the interaction in person. Heather contributes most of the talk, while the teacher's contribution is limited to just three turns: a response to Heather's question about the nature of the student's fluency ("It was choppy and word by word"); a summing up of Heather's coaching ("So you're saying I should be quiet while she's rereading a familiar book"); and a suggested approach to the situation ("I could just let her go ahead and read"). There is not much in the way of collaboration or inquiry in this interaction. The coach's intent does not appear to be to support the teacher's inquiry, but rather to tell the teacher what to do and how to do it.

The shift in understanding and teaching that Heather is working toward—that the student's phrased reading can be improved if the teacher uses small cards to show where the phrases are within the text—was not clearly communicated. Why not? While Heather was demonstrating to the teacher how to frame the phrases, the teacher was looking away, writing a few notes about something Heather had said that she wanted to remember. In fact, despite Heather's clear demonstration of how to explicitly teach the student to read in a phrased way, the teacher wrongly concluded that Heather's point was not to talk during the familiar rereading and just let the student read.

Heather tried to be collaborative at this point by asking the teacher, "What do you think?" but that was not the right time for collaborative inquiry. The teacher has clearly misunderstood the point of Heather's coaching (likely because her attention was elsewhere while Heather was demonstrating the instructional procedure), and Heather's asking, "What do you think?" at this point is not going to help get things back on track. In fact, the question comes across as an attempt to foster agreement with the coach's view rather than to foster inquiry. Now, instead of framing the phrases in the story to support the student's fluency as Heather was coaching her to do, the teacher will likely let the student read without interruption or teaching. In fact, the teacher has decided to assess phrasing from now on ("see what she does on her own") even though coach and teacher already agree that the student's reading is choppy and not fluent. The student needs to be taught, not assessed. The shift needed in teaching is not clear.

Debriefing a Coaching Session. Afterward, Emily and Heather worked
together to debrief the coaching. Heather had not picked up on the mismatch in understanding about teaching for phrasing, but she did analyze
that she had done most of the talking during the coaching session. As a
result of Emily and Heather's discussion, Heather set the following coaching goals for the next school visit to a different teacher:

- Instead of questioning the teacher and then telling, pose a
  question and then look for evidence from the lesson together.
  Involve the teacher in looking for that evidence. A good
  opportunity for Heather to do this came following the teacher's
  description of the student's reading as choppy and word by
  word. Heather could have asked the teacher to go back and
  find a few instances in the story where this was the case. By
  looking for evidence together, both Heather and the teacher
  would be engaged in collaborative inquiry, each being tentative
  about their theory while they looked for evidence to support
  the hypothesis about the student's fluency. The coach becomes
  a co-learner. Once they collected evidence they could decide
  together whether the student's reading really wasn't fluent.
  Together they could then think about how to teach the student
  to read in a more phrased way. Heather's demonstration would
  have been well positioned at this point to make a difference in
  understanding and thinking.
- Ask the teacher to try the procedure herself. Heather and
  the teacher could have brought the student back for a few
  minutes of quick teaching, or Heather could have taken
  the role of the student and the teacher could have tried the
  teaching with her. In either case, Heather would be providing
  the teacher with an opportunity to try out the teaching
  procedure herself, and in doing so, the teacher would have
  already been participating differently in the activity of
  teaching students to read in a phrased way. This change in
  participation in an activity is the goal of coaching according
  to our understanding of learning. It is up to the coach to
  organize the experience so that the teacher has an opportunity
  to participate differently.
- Give the teacher more time and space to take notes while
  debriefing. This means waiting without talking while the
  teacher makes a few notes. The notes need not be extensive
  or take a long time to write, but because they will serve as an
  important memory prompt later when the coach is no longer

present to provide support, it is important that the teacher have a chance to make them during the debriefing without missing any new information.

- Wait for the teacher to be ready to participate in the inquiry before moving on with your agenda. If the coach invests time to demonstrate an instructional procedure, it must be considered an important understanding to sort out. In this case the teacher couldn't pay attention because she was busy writing quick notes to herself. Her attention was divided and she missed the point of the coaching.

A Subsequent Coaching Session. During Heather's second coaching session later that day, the teacher she was observing finished teaching well before the allotted time. She could have taught the student for 10 more minutes, but decided not to use that time for instruction. Notice that the important issue that emerges as they discuss the lesson afterward is not that there was unused extra time, but that the writing instruction could be more robust. Also notice the change in talk. This interaction looks and sounds more like collaborative inquiry.

HEATHER: What would you like to talk about first?

TEACHER: Well, I know I had more time to teach, but I had finished everything I wanted to cover and I didn't want to do anything else. If we're supposed to follow the child and individualize instruction, there didn't seem to be anything else to do. [Pause–seeming to give the coach a turn to talk. No comment from the coach.] I noticed the writing went a lot quicker than the reading. I could spend more time on writing.

HEATHER: [Looking back through student's writing journal.] I see that when she writes a story it's often about her.

TEACHER: Yes, she often puts herself in the story . . . so I should play her up more in the stories!

HEATHER: Let's see how that might work. Today she read *Nick's Glasses.*

TEACHER: I could say, "Nick couldn't find his glasses anywhere in the story you read today. Have you ever lost anything like Nick? What did you do to try and find it?"

HEATHER: You probably will get a more elaborate, richer story that way, with more opportunities for her to learn about writing. You'll need more time for instruction then, won't you! Let's get the student to come back and you can try writing another story.

Heather's question, "What would you like to talk about first?" was a genuine one. Heather told me later that she wasn't sure how to start the coaching session and decided to ask the teacher what she wanted to talk about first. The most interesting part of the exchange was the teacher's pause after her comment that she didn't think there was anything else to work on so she finished the lesson early. With that pause, the teacher looked at Heather. All the signals suggested that it was Heather's turn to say something. When Heather didn't say anything, the teacher continued with her analysis and went straight to the heart of the matter: that she could spend more time on writing.

Heather's silence didn't seem rude; it lasted for only a few seconds, and it appeared as though she was giving the teacher a few more moments to analyze and reflect on her own. It would have been so easy for Heather to step in at that point and start talking, perhaps in a very didactic way ("Yes, you're right, now here's how you do that"), but she didn't. By giving the teacher some time and space for analysis, the coaching interaction became more collaborative. A quick glance at the amount of teacher talk in this interaction provides the evidence that this time, the coach and teacher are problem solving together and have a shared focus and understanding.

Adopting a Co-Learner Stance. In this next example, Arwa, the coach, adopts that same co-learner stance that Heather did in the second example. As you read this interaction, note Arwa's invitational stance and the way she includes the teacher as her collaborator in the inquiry. Arwa poses questions that she herself can't answer, she wonders about things, and she clearly communicates that stance to the teacher.

ARWA: What did you think about the new book that he read for the first time? I wonder if it was too easy?

TEACHER: Well, he had trouble with a few words like . . . [Teacher turns pages and looks through the book.]

ARWA: [Looking at her notes.] He said *web* for *wind*.

TEACHER: I think I said, "Try that again" and he said, "web."

ARWA: [Referring to her notes.] Yes, you said that, but before you said that, you said, "It could be *web*, but look at the last part of that word." Then you told him to go back and try that again.

TEACHER: Uhm. What I actually said was more helpful because I found the error for him when I said, "It could be *web*." That was telling him where the error was. I didn't solve it for him, though: I didn't tell him what the word was, but I did take him straight to the error. Maybe I'm giving him too much help. He probably needs to monitor and notice the errors on his own.

ARWA: Noticing the error is important. That would be a strategic action. Let's think back to how you helped him when he encountered difficulty at other times. Maybe you are the one who usually does the monitoring for him. [Coach looks back through her notes while the teacher looks through the books that were read.]

TEACHER: I think I'm usually telling him where the errors are. Sometimes he would notice an error by himself, but when he didn't notice and kept on reading, I would come in and tell him, "It could be that word."

ARWA: I've got that in my notes too. It's good that he does notice his errors sometimes. When he doesn't though, what could you say instead that would help him find the error?

TEACHER: I could say, "You need to read that again and look very carefully this time."

ARWA: Then he'll have to find the error on his own.

TEACHER: OK, so let's say I tell him to go back and look carefully, and he still doesn't notice the error. What do I do then?

ARWA: You could give him more help then.

TEACHER: Yeah, that's when I could say, "It could be *web* but look at the end of the word too." So I've found it for him now, but at least I didn't come in with the most amount of help first. And I'm teaching him how to look, what to notice.

Arwa was genuinely puzzled about whether the book the student was reading was too easy, and she posed the question so that she and the teacher could consider it together. This is a wise move. After all, the teacher has much more knowledge about the student than Arwa can collect in a relatively brief observation of teaching. Perhaps more important, though, Arwa's question serves to reveal her tentative stance; she seems to be saying, "Help me think this through." As such, the question becomes an invitation to the teacher to inquire together with Arwa.

Arwa and the teacher clearly listen to one another. Each response is connected to a comment that came before. They are keeping on with the inquiry together. Their exploring leads them to hypothesize that perhaps the teacher is finding the student's errors for him, rather than supporting him to monitor his reading independently. This occurred when the teacher realized that when the student read the word *web* for *wind*, she told him, "Yes, that could be *web*." She wasn't aware that she was usually interacting with the student in this way when errors occurred. In order to help the student monitor while reading, she analyzed that she could simply say, "Try that again." This teaching requires the student to find the error and teaches the student to monitor while reading.

The other notable part of this interaction is that Arwa looked back through her notes for examples of how the teacher supported the student having difficulty, while the teacher looked through the books they had read and reflected on her teaching. It is possible that Arwa had more examples of similar interactions at her fingertips, but instead of telling the teacher, she waited and gave the teacher time to analyze and reflect.

This coaching interaction also contains examples of both the coach and the teacher posing questions, another hallmark of collaborative inquiry. When the teacher analyzed that it might be more powerful to have the student find the error independently, she then raised the question, "What do I do if he still doesn't notice the error?" The coach followed this new line of inquiry posed by the teacher and supported the teacher in sorting this out.

Both Arwa and Heather are guiding teachers to collaborate with them in the inquiry. It's easy to see where the coaching might have got off track, though. As Lindfors (1999) notes, acts of inquiry should be handled with care because it's easy to offend with questions (p. 194). Let's look next at some principles of guiding effective coaching conversations that can be derived from these examples.

PRINCIPLES OF EFFECTIVE COACHING CONVERSATIONS

We have emphasized in this chapter the important role of language in supporting learning. We probably know this intuitively. If you have ever changed your opinion midstream in a conversation, answered your own question just as you were posing it to someone else, discussed a problem with someone to help make a decision, or talked yourself through a sequence of steps to help your recall, you know the power of language to support and extend thinking. It follows, then, that a primary role of the coach is to guide collaborative inquiry, which might take place between the coach and teacher working together or between the coach and a group of teachers.

Our examples of coaches working with teachers demonstrate the challenge of guiding effective coaching conversations. It seems easy to lapse into telling, yet as we know, mandates that involve skillful teaching and decision making are likely to fail. Several principles of guiding teacher inquiry for literacy learning that follow from our discussion include the following:

- *Adopt a co-learner stance.* It helps sometimes to start a sentence with "I wonder why" or "I wonder if." This wondering aloud provides a model for the teacher to adopt a similar tentative, investigative stance; sends the message that the coach really is a co-learner; clearly reveals the complexity of the work; and shows clearly that the coach is not the sole authority when it comes to skillful teaching and decision making.
- *Provide a forum for inquiry whereby teachers can examine principles of instruction and suggest alternative teaching moves.* Creating a forum is more about establishing a setting for the co-construction of learning in which teachers are encouraged to share, question, and revise opinions (see Wells, 1999). The coach's affective stance is probably the most influential element in establishing this forum; after all, emotions play a primary role in learning (Lyons, 2003). Our review of effective coaches presented earlier in this chapter included descriptors such as *respectful of others' knowledge, good listeners, passionate, empathetic* (NCTE, 2004, p. 1), *reflective,* and *have a good sense of humor* (Dole, 2004).
- *Use collaborative inquiry as the mechanism to provide feedback, facilitate reflection, and foster change.* Teachers need to know the principles of collaborative inquiry in order to participate, so the coach should explain them before starting their shared inquiry.

Despite this focus on collaborative inquiry to support skillful teaching, we include the caveat that the coach should not rely on talk alone as evidence of change in teaching practices, as David Cohen (1990) demonstrated with his study of Mrs. Oublier, a sixth-grade math teacher. She spoke enthusiastically and knowledgeably about a shift in instruction, but observation of her teaching showed that her participation in the practice did not change. This notion of a shift in participation, you will recall from earlier in this chapter, provided the foundation for our definition of learning. Phyllis, a literacy coach, wrote about this in her reflection about the value of visiting teachers to observe them teach. She wrote, "I get to know the teacher more in depth and can tell if the teacher is just able to 'talk the talk' or if she can really execute it."

CONCLUSION

There will be times when the coach has to mandate change and tell what needs to be done, but these will involve surface-level kinds of changes that do not require skillful thinking and decision making. We think the challenge for coaches may lie in the other end of the continuum: guiding teachers in collaborative inquiry. This is challenging work, as our examples demonstrate. We offer the following thoughts in conclusion:

- Look for changes in participation in an activity, not just enthusiasm for change. It's not enough to embrace change.
- Provide support along with the pressure for change. Mary Fried, a colleague of ours, quotes Fullan (1993), who says that pressure is necessary for change to occur; but along with the need for pressure, Mary adds that support is also required. Pressure to change teaching, along with coaching for support, will result in change. After all, tall buildings remain standing because the steel girders counteract the pressure of the concrete. Without the support of the girders, the pressure wins and the building collapses. If there's pressure without support, change will fail.
- Work together with teachers to build knowledge collaboratively. This kind of co-learner stance can provide motivation for learning (Wells, 1999).
- Start with the most powerful questions, such as "Why . . . ?" or "What else . . . ?" or "What evidence is there . . . ?" These questions establish a genuine co-learner stance and are invitations to the teacher to be a partner in the inquiry.

We have considered in this chapter the role of the literacy coach in guiding teachers' collaborative inquiry. In the following chapter we describe what coaches can do to create the kinds of contexts that will foster collaborative inquiry.

CHAPTER 3

Creating Contexts for Coaching Conversations

In the Introduction we described a friend and colleague who was talking to us about coaching teachers. One of her questions to us was, "What can I do?" This would seem to be a simple question. It is a question that seems to invite the response, "Well, do X, Y, and Z" or "Do A, B, and C." In our work coaching teachers and working with coaches, we have learned the response to "What can I do?" is far more complex. This is helpful to learn because it suggests to us that there are many varied ways that educators can work on the coaching enterprise. In fact, as a profession we probably have yet to explore very many of them. For us, as educators, there are different ways we can explore the question of what we can do: from craft approaches, to case studies, to experiments; and we think the question of what we can do is one that may be around for a very long time, with fruitful results.

In this book we have actually broken down our friend's question into a number of subquestions. When we began with the question, "What can I do?" one subquestion we posed was, "What contexts have we created to consider coaching?" A second question that came to us was, "How do we as coaches observe teaching?" A third question that came on the heels of the first and second was, "After working in a particular context observing teaching, how do we guide the debriefing of the teaching?" In this chapter we discuss contexts for coaching.

Creating a context to coach teachers is a critical element in building the capacity for educators to study their teaching, consider what is working well, estimate what might work better, determine future courses of action, and implement change with the goal of supporting student learning in an even more powerful way. We begin by discussing the context for coaching and then explain how a coach can maintain this context using different groupings of the participants.

CREATING A CONTEXT FOR COACHING

As teacher educators we often use the concepts of knowledge, skill, and disposition to discuss preservice and inservice teacher preparation. As we cited in chapter 2, when Dole (2004) asked a group of successful coaches what makes an effective reading coach, they suggested reading expertise (knowledge), successful teaching experience (skill), reflectivity (skill and disposition), articulation of observation (knowledge and skill), ability to support (skill), planning on the run (skill), and humor (disposition). We can see from this list that knowledge and skills figure prominently, while the dispositions of the coach and the teachers being coached get less attention.

Emotions and Coaching

We have noticed that when educators describe the coaching context—or the characteristics that describe the circumstances under which coaching participants undertake their work—they often use emotion-laden words. We agree with Dole (2004) that good humor is an important element in a coaching relationship, but it takes more than good wit to support teaching and learning. In the following sections we consider the affective dimensions of learning.

Emotions and Child Learning. The work of our colleague Carol Lyons (1999, 2003) on emotions and child learning has been very useful to us in thinking about adult learning in the coaching context. In discussing child learning, Lyons (1999) explains that "parts of the brain and nervous system that deal with emotional regulation play a crucial role in planning, discriminating, and choosing between alternatives, monitoring, self-correcting, and regulating one's behavior" (p. 73). We would argue that certainly the same could be said of adult behavior. The emotional state of both the coach and the teacher has a direct influence on the coaching context, in terms of what gets taught and how it gets taught. If we acknowledge this, then we must consider the *effect of affect* on teaching and learning in the coaching context.

Lyons (1999) is able to offer some assistance to us here. When writing about brain research and a part of the brain known as the reticular activating system (RAS), or the part that helps focus attention, Lyons explains:

> Feeling successful is critical in keeping the RAS open. The RAS must be opened and aroused in order for the child to attend; without attention the child will not learn. Having a positive, non-threatening, non-stressful experience while learning enhances the child's opportunity for success. (p. 78)

This finding is very important for the work of coaches because it suggests that it is essential to coach in a nonstressful setting.

Emily had an interesting experience as an adult that illustrates a piece of this complex dilemma. She had earned her driver's license in her late teens and had driven around small towns and large cities in Canada and in large cities overseas. When she immigrated to the United States, the state motor vehicle agency would not transfer her Canadian driver's license and required that she complete both the written and road tests. Part of the road test required maneuvering a car through a series of traffic cones following the directions of a driver examiner. This was actually an easier test than the one that she had passed as a Canadian driver years before; that test required rear-angle and parallel parking in a space lined with traffic cones. In the U.S. test she was permitted to even hit the traffic cones but not topple them; whereas in Canada even touching a cone with the car meant immediate failure.

One would think that Emily would not even need to prepare for such a test after having successfully driven for so many years, but the opposite was true. Each time Emily went to practice for her test, she grew worse rather than better! She even concluded that she could not drive at all and that she would have to take taxis. When the big day came for the exam, she completed the test successfully, narrowly averting disaster when she touched a cone with the rear fender, making the cone rock from side to side before coming to rest. Then, when she returned home with her Ohio driver's license in hand, she nimbly rear-angle parked her large car by delicately maneuvering around the bicycle and lawnmower in her narrow garage.

What was interesting about this experience for Emily was that the high stakes led her to want to attend to her driving, but the pressure of failure meant not only that she could not attend to her driving, but that the most basic of tasks was almost impossible. And this was a case where Emily was not learning a new task, but was being asked to demonstrate a task she had performed successfully for years. Once the test was passed and the stress was gone, she was able to go home and complete a far more intricate maneuver than the one required on the driver's test. We can conclude that emotions play a role in one's ability to learn and participate in activities. Anxiety and stress impede learning and can even prevent someone from carrying out a familiar task.

Thus it is important that coaches consider the role of emotions in learning and create supportive contexts. In writing about how teachers can teach children, Lyons (1999) found that teachers can

> create an instructional environment that includes two major features to help the child feel positive and successful. First, they teach the child the

task. Second, they keep the task easy so that the child will feel successful and will attend to the process. (p. 78)

We argue that the coach can create a context for effective coaching by doing the same things. First, teach the task. This can be a particular teaching task such as introducing a new book to students, or it can be an assessment task such as taking a running record (see Clay, 2002). A very helpful task to teach might be one that contributes to renewal in teaching, such as teaching an approach for teacher self-examination. Second, keep the task easy enough to ensure success. This is especially important in schools in which there is considerable pressure to change test scores overnight. The coach needs to support teachers in setting achievable goals in the initial months and years of coaching, so that teachers can build on initial success to realize later success.

Emotions and Adult Learning. Although Lyons (1999) provides us with a useful starting point by discussing emotion and child learning, we would suggest that emotions may be even more important for adult learners because they have many more prior experiences than a child has. Dirkx (2001) offers a useful summary of the research on adult learning:

> The literature underscores the importance of attending to emotions and feelings in contexts, interactions, and relationships that characterize adult learning. . . . [The literature suggests that] emotion and feelings are deeply intertwined with perceiving and processing information from our external environments, storing and retrieving information in memory, reasoning, and the embodiment of learning. (p. 68)

This work has important implications for our work in coaching teachers. Recently, Adrian was teaching a class about literacy in the social setting. By the third week a number of the teachers were literally in tears. They liked the class and loved the assignments, which required that they interview and observe the students they taught each day and that they have a conversation with parents, preferably at the parents' homes. Yet the teachers explained that the documentation for those activities (which consisted of three short papers) was impossible for them to complete. In trying to meet their teaching requirements, they were barely able to make it to class. While they could collect most of the data for the assignments during the school day, they simply did not have the time to write up what they had learned.

This was disappointing to Adrian. On the one hand, he reasoned that the rigor of the course demanded the assignment requirement. "Should I say, 'Toughen up'?" he wondered. On the other hand, even the most basic understanding of Maslow's Hierarchy of Needs would suggest that these teachers could not advance in their learning under such intense pressure. Working together to identify that the problem was one of time to document learning, Adrian and his students created a number of options that reduced the stress. The teachers had the choice of sharing what they had learned in a class presentation, in a paper, or in a personal interview with Adrian. Interestingly, about one third of the students still chose the paper; one third chose the class presentation; and one third chose the personal interview. Adrian even received e-mailed thank you notes from students saying how much they appreciated the flexibility. Most important, Adrian felt he learned even more from the range of presentations and that he understood student learning in an even more powerful way, especially through the interview option. We can conclude that both coach and teacher may experience a range of emotions, but through careful problem solving we can have more potent learning for both.

Building the Context for Coaching

Once the coach acknowledges the importance of emotion in adult learning, this knowledge can be used to make instructional choices that are purposeful efforts to build the coaching context. One essential element of this context is the recognition that each teacher and the coach are equals in the coaching context. In such a context, each participant has an equal opportunity to talk, to pose questions, and to challenge the opinions of others. Since creating a context in which participants are emotionally ready to learn is essential, Emily has proposed that sitting in a circle, without having desks in front of the participants, is a recognition of equal membership (E. Rodgers, 2000a). Emily explains:

> There is no "head of a table" in a circle . . . and therefore, no one holds more right to talk than anyone else. Any other formation, including a circle with a table, automatically sets someone apart as the *leader* of the discussion. In circle discussions little need exists to acknowledge a single person as having the most capability of extending the learning of others. (p. 7)

Emily also explains that with the right of equality also comes the "responsibility to articulate ideas, to actively try to understand each other, to follow a line of inquiry started by someone else and to stay with it" (p. 7).

A second approach that we have discussed in our coaching work has been the recognition that teachers, rather than the coach, need to take ownership in creating questions about their own teaching and in answering these questions (A. Rodgers, 2002). As Adrian has explained,

Teacher ownership dramatically changes the way teacher education research can be represented. In the future, teams of teachers and researchers
will need to study what happens when they mutually construct research
questions, when they overlap teaching and researching responsibilities,
and when they consider multiple ways of representing data. (p. 156)

Researching our own teaching and coaching in the coaching context is a
good way to begin this line of teacher and researcher inquiry.

We have found that while the articulation of a quality coaching context is challenging, it is essential to conduct quality coaching. Fostering a
problem-solving relationship—not where children are the problem, but
rather where we create challenges we wish to address—can be helpful in
creating a quality coaching context. To some degree, the coach needs to
create a social event (and the occasional social event at someone's house
can be helpful, too) so that each participant can see the other teachers and
the coach as well-rounded individuals who have come to teaching to support student learning. Although the role of the coach is not to be a caterer
of snacks and meals, the coach can take some ownership of setting a social ambience in which teachers can work together in helping each other
address professional problems. As Strickland (2004) concluded, when it
comes to creating the coaching context, the coach is a leader, not a supervisor; a supporter of self-reflection and self-assessment, not an evaluator;
and a partner of the principal, not a snoop for the principal.

GROUPING TEACHERS
TO FOSTER COACHING CONVERSATIONS

In this section we discuss the kinds of groups that coaches can create to
support the coaching enterprise and the kind of work that can be undertaken in those groups. It is interesting to us that when educators think
about coaching, they automatically think about the work that might be
undertaken in a group. This suggests that Vygotsky (1978) was indeed
right when he wrote that "human learning presupposes a specific social
nature" (p. 88). What we would like to do in this section is not only offer
suggestions for the kinds of groups that coaches can contrive to accomplish coaching work, but also reconsider the idea of what exactly consti-
tutes a group in coaching. We think that there is a range of social groupings that can be used to accomplish the tasks of coaching; what the good
literacy coach does is right-size the number and constituents so that the
group is aligned with the coaching task that the literacy coach has set
out to accomplish. Additionally, we suggest that while some groups may
have the same participants in it over time, in other cases the literacy

coach may periodically change the constituents over time to assist in right-sizing the group.

Focusing the Goal of Coaching:
Using Groups to Foster Particular Kinds of Inquiry into Teaching

Perhaps because educators have received most of their training in a university setting, many think of coaching as a task that is undertaken as a whole group at regular intervals. In other words, some educators may think of coaching as something similar to a university class meeting that meets perhaps weekly for a predetermined length of time. Occasionally, some educators have a twist on this view. Educators might think about coaching as an event in which the coach comes to a classroom (perhaps once a week) to observe teaching. After the observation, the coach may sit with a teacher and discuss the lesson. Perhaps based on this observation, the coach may have a few suggestions, questions, clarifications, observations, or commiserations. The coaching episode is then over, and the teacher chooses which, if any, suggestions to act on. While the observations may be useful and the commiseration helps a teacher feel that other teachers face the same challenges, it is unclear how the group meetings or class visits help a teacher proceed and improve his or her teaching.

In our work as coaches, we have found that it is helpful if we carefully consider the goals that we want to achieve as a coach. Once we have determined them, we can then decide how we might group teachers in a way that supports their achievement. In some cases, our grouping options are limited. For example, in our work with preservice teachers in a university seminar on student teaching, the university system requires that we meet weekly as a group. We have the option to do some things, such as break the entire class into smaller groups, but we do not have the freedom to tailor the groups and size in an entirely free way. Likewise, when we are working with inservice teachers and their students have been dismissed early on the first Monday of every month for teacher professional development, we are also limited in the way we can group the teachers. What these limitations on grouping suggest to us is not that we should give up and only work with teachers in whole groups or break-outs, but rather that we should think about

- The kind of scheduling of whole-group meetings that we should seek from administrators
- The kind of work that can be accomplished in the whole group or in break-out groups
- The kind of work that can be accomplished in groups or individually outside the scheduled meetings of a whole group

Scheduling Time to Work Together. Many educators have written about the lack of time during the school day for professional development, especially in the U.S. and Canadian context (Fullan & Hargreaves, 1996; Lewis, Perry, & Murata, 2006; Tharp & Gallimore, 1988). Not surprisingly, some educators have responded by working very hard to schedule time in the school day to create such professional development opportunities. For example, a 1985 study by Grimmett, Moody, and Balasubramaniam (cited in Tharp & Gallimore, 1988) found that the most successful use of coaching occurred in a school where the "principal arranged a series of interconnected activity settings: he himself substituted for teachers, taking more than one class at a time to the gym, so that the teachers could actually meet!" (p. 201). What is interesting to us is that while this quote may be 20 years old, it could very well have been written today. As a profession, coaching has not come very far from this kind of support for creating coaching settings, where educators largely rely on the good graces of a fellow staff member, or administrator, or on an early dismissal where we cram a number of required professional tasks into a late afternoon.

What we would suggest is that by virtue of their creating a literacy coach position, schools and school districts have some buy-in to the concept of the coaching experience. Therefore it is important that coaches work with administrators to also create time in the school day when this coaching experience is to take place. The coach will also want to think about what groups of teachers he or she will want to work with. For example, should the coach suggest to the administrator that all second-grade teachers be free from teaching at a particular time? This would work well if the coach wished to work with all second-grade teachers at once, but in some cases the coach may wish to work with teachers across grade levels. Therefore the coach will want to give some thought to who would be the optimal members to attend a large group meeting and how these larger group meetings will be scheduled.

The difficulty of obtaining time also suggests how respectful we must be of that time. Given how hard group-meeting time is to come by in the first place, it is essential that coaches not lose the time they do have in efforts that are not directly related to the coaching enterprise. One task that the coach will need to undertake is to screen out the unwanted noise in the system that can be handled in other ways. Many of us have attended meetings where lengthy announcements are made, where the chair of a meeting spends considerable time reading some text to us that could have been distributed to be read prior to the meeting, or where a small group of individuals have a lot to say about some initiative that is of tangential interest to the other participants. It is in the whole-group setting that the literacy coach must work hard to respect this precious time by using memos, distributing readings ahead of time, and using subgroups or sub-committees, so that the meeting can be focused on coaching rather than administering.

Coaching in the Whole-Group Setting. While much coaching can take place outside the whole-group context, the whole-group meeting does have a number of important roles to play. One is that it provides an opportunity for the coach to focus the attention of teachers on a particular task. With the increased pressure brought by calls for accountability, teachers feel stretched, pulled, and twisted in different directions. The power of the whole-group meeting is that it provides the coach with a way of focusing everyone on one objective. In some cases it may be a very tangible objective such as increasing the number of students passing a proficiency test. In other cases the objective may be to seek explanations, such as wondering what kinds of instruction we could provide so that students would be better able to respond to a prompt such as "Find the main point in the paragraph." In still other cases the objective may be to share data and interpret it, such as when proficiency results are returned to the school and the students have increased their performance on a standardized test.

In these brief examples that we have provided, we use illustrations from testing situations exclusively. But a much more powerful example was provided to us recently when we worked with Mary Fried, a highly respected master teacher and a clinical faculty member for many years at The Ohio State University. Mary had been invited to work with three literacy coaches at a nearby school district to support them in their coaching role. Throughout the school year, Mary worked directly with the teachers and then debriefed her coaching afterward with the three literacy coaches. In the first whole-group meeting Mary began her work by asking teachers what challenges their students faced. After providing a few minutes for teachers to think about the question, Mary went around the group to hear the responses. Although the responses differed, there was one thing that all teachers had in common: They all focused on the characteristics of the students or their homes. One teacher responded that literacy was not valued in the home. Another responded that literacy was valued in the home, but there were not very many sources of print. A third teacher responded that the parents worked regularly with their child, but the child did not seem to respond. Perhaps the child had difficulty processing instruction, the teacher ventured.

What interested us was how Mary handled the situation. Instead of challenging the claims, she tried a slight variation on the question. This time she asked, "What challenges does school instruction pose for your students?" Again the teachers thought about the question. After a time, they gave their responses. One teacher responded that the kindergarten teacher had not equipped his students to perform in first grade. Another responded that the children were not ready to read. A third teacher responded that she worked regularly with a child, but he did not seem to respond. Perhaps the child had difficulty processing instruction, the teacher offered.

Again, instead of challenging the claims, Mary made one statement and posed a third question:

> It may well be that there is a lack of print material in the home or that there is a surplus of print in the home. It may well be that the child does not respond to the parent instruction or that he does. It may well be that the kindergarten teacher did not prepare the child for first grade or that she did. And it may well be that the child is not ready to read, or that he is. I have many thoughts on what you have said, but in reality, for our purposes, it really does not matter. All of the factors you have mentioned are simply outside of our control. While it may be interesting to discuss them, discussing them will not help us in our teaching of the child because we are powerless to address the factors you mentioned. In fact, the only thing that we can be sure of, the only thing that we can control, is our own teaching. You have invited me here today because you are hoping that I can help you think about your teaching. Your district perceives that some of the students are struggling and that if we look carefully, we may be able to help them in an even more powerful way than we have done in the past. It is not that there is something wrong with our teaching. But rather, the question is how can we help students continue to move forward? Let me ask a third question: What is something you can change about your teaching that may help your students learn in an even more powerful way than before?

This time the responses were very different. In using this prompt Mary solicited a range of responses, all of them focused on teaching and factors that were within the control of the teacher. It was from this point that Mary was able to focus the attention of both teachers and coaches on what could be changed in the teaching of students to support learning in an even better way. Through this initial meeting and subsequent periodic whole-group meetings and smaller-group work, Mary was able to hold the focus of the entire group for the entire year on how they could examine their own teaching so that they could teach in an even more potent way.

There are a number of different directions in which a literacy coach can focus the attention of teachers. In Mary's case, she chose to initially focus the attention of teachers on how they could change their teaching. In addition to *studying teaching*, literacy coaches could also focus the attention of teachers on *how they can conduct inquiry* into teaching. For example, we have seen some literacy coaches focus the attention of teachers with whom they worked by asking the teachers to undertake a case study of one student. Other coaches we have observed have asked teachers to use an action research approach, whereby the teachers use an inquiry structure to document what occurs when a teacher makes a change in the way he or she teaches.

In other settings we have observed, especially in those where teachers are quite adept at tinkering with their instruction, some literacy coaches we have observed have spent a lot of time relating in whole-group sessions how teachers might *document their teaching*. This can be especially useful if teachers are undertaking advanced certification, such as National Board Certification (www.nbpts.org), or have chosen to discuss their work at professional teaching conferences, such as those hosted by the IRA (www.ira.org), the NCTE (www.ncte.org), or the NAEYC (www.naeyc.org). Another possibility for the whole-group setting is the modeling of teaching strategies. Sometimes this modeling may take the form of sharing a videotape. In other cases, the coach may act as a teacher and model a strategy, either by bringing a student or students into the whole-group session or by asking a teacher or teachers to play the role of students. Finally, we have also observed literacy coaches work in whole-group sessions on supporting teachers in evaluating their own teaching. We stress here that when we use the word *evaluating*, we do not mean making summative evaluations for the purpose of hiring, firing, or compensating teachers. Instead, we mean that coaches can assist and support teachers by helping them evaluate their own work. Much of this work is begun in smaller groups, often in one-to-one consultation between coach and teacher or teacher and peer, but this work can be continued in the whole-group session. It is in the whole-group session that coaches can discuss the purpose of evaluating one's own teaching or the use of instruments and rubrics that can assist teachers in evaluating their own work. (See Chapter 4 for a more detailed discussion of rubrics.)

In addition to focusing and retaining the attention of the whole group on a particular problem, the other opportunity offered through a whole-group meeting is sharing how teachers have responded to the coaching. As Tharp and Gallimore (1988) have found that "to develop competencies and programs, . . . it is essential that teachers have supportive interaction with peers" (p. 191). One venue in which peers can demonstrate challenges they are facing is in the whole-group session. During the middle of the school year, teachers might bring case study materials back to the whole group, where they can be analyzed. Some of these case materials may take the form of videotapes of teaching, lesson plans, running records, or student work. At the end of a semester or the end of the school year, teachers might share their work on a particular case. At a time like this, they might share a collection of artifacts that document their teaching. Using these artifacts, teachers can view their own teaching through multiple lenses and can learn from each other about the challenge of changing teaching. (For more discussion on lenses, see Chapter 4.)

Working Within a Context

Although whole-group meetings are essential for supporting a school-wide coaching effort, much of the work of the coach can be undertaken outside the whole-group meeting context. One way to do this is to work in small groups to establish a spiral of inquiry.

Small-Group Work: Establishing a Spiral of Inquiry. Through working in small groups, in pairs, in one-to-one settings with the coach, and in one-to-one settings with fellow teachers, the power of coaching can be felt. This is especially true because the observation or modeling of teaching followed by discussion can help establish a *spiral of inquiry* that supports teachers not only in understanding teaching decisions, but also in acting on what they have observed. Additionally, we should point out that while the focus of this book is on the conversations that occur between coach and teacher, it is not as if these conversations occurred in a vacuum. There may be other teachers working at the school who are not working with the literacy coach. In the following few paragraphs we talk principally about how teachers working with the coach can work in small groups and pairs, but it can be important for the teachers working with a coach to talk to other teachers not working with the coach. To distinguish between these two groups, we are going to use the phrase *in-network teachers* to describe teachers working with the literacy coach, and *out-of-network teachers* to describe the teachers not working with the literacy coach, but who may be colleagues of the in-network teachers.

One of the challenges of the whole-group setting is that we typically cannot observe actual teaching with 15 or 20 teachers present in the class. In fact, in the whole-group setting it is more likely that we will observe representations of teaching using things such as videotapes, student artifacts, lesson plans, or lesson records. The power of smaller groupings is that we can actually observe teaching. The use of small groupings can occur in two ways:

1. *Teaching observations can be conducted in small groups.* Two or three teachers could attend a class taught by one of their peers. In other cases, teachers might sit in an observation room separated from the teaching space by a one-way mirror and observe the work of their peer.
2. *Teaching observations can be undertaken in one-to-one settings.* In these cases the coach might watch a teacher teach; a teacher who is being coached might watch a fellow teacher who is being coached; or an in-network teacher might watch an out-of-network teacher, and vice versa.

In all these cases, teachers will want to undertake a prebriefing, an observation, and a debriefing. In the prebriefing, observers can discuss with the teacher the subject of the lesson being observed and the approach being used. This discussion is essential in supporting quality interpretation by the observers of the lesson. Especially in a coaching setting, teachers may be attempting an alternative teaching approach. If observers are not aware of this, they may inadvertently counsel the teacher back toward a traditional approach.

During the observation, teachers will want to take notes regarding what they observe. These notes may take the form of a script in which the words of teacher and students are recorded. Other teachers may make procedural, theoretical, hypothetical, or methodological notes. Additionally, if the teaching being observed is taking place behind a one-way mirror, teachers and coach have the opportunity to discuss the teaching as it unfolds. It is in this setting that it is incumbent on the coach to look for nuances in the teaching that may not be observed by the teacher-observers and to push teachers to look for and comment on what they might otherwise miss.

Finally, subsequent to the teaching, the observers can debrief with the teacher following the lesson. In this setting, observers can clarify questions that arose during the observation; they can follow up on things they may have observed; and they can probe the teacher about why the specific instructional choices were made. In addition to these tasks, it is also important that if a literacy coach is present at the observation, he or she should prompt both the observers and the observed teacher to take their conclusions and use them to change their teaching in the following lesson. It is this prompting that helps promote a spiral of inquiry so that teachers can make changes in their own teaching.

Sharing Small-Group Learnings with the Whole Group. Because of the way this chapter has been structured, it may seem that the literacy coach should begin with a whole-group setting and then continue in a small-group setting. We suggest that what is learned in the smaller groups can be documented and then brought back to the whole group for further consideration. Up to this point, the central role of the coach has been either to lead discussion with teachers or to foster discussion by teachers about what is observed. Yet the literacy coach can also observe many teachers working in different settings. Because of this the coach has the ability to collect the most illustrative examples of a problem or issue being explored by teachers. We believe that a powerful way coaches can use small groups is to gather artifacts from teachers and then assemble different artifacts to create a protocol that can be explored by the whole group.

A *protocol* represents a range of artifacts that document a hypothetical case. Some artifacts may be real ones, while others may be created by the coach for the purpose of illustration. These artifacts are then combined to create a case that illustrates issues or problems faced by a number of students. In addition to presenting these case materials to teachers, the literacy coach can provide procedures for working through the case materials. These procedures may mean that some teachers undertake additional research, while others test teaching possibilities in their class, and still others study the case materials to obtain further insights. We think that while it is essential that teachers study their own teaching of their own students, there is also power in coaches using pieces of different cases to assemble a protocol to lead teachers in their learning.

CONCLUSION

In this chapter we have discussed the importance of thinking about the context in which coaching can occur and the groupings that support that context. We summarize these groupings in Figure 3.1. In the left-hand column we define the kind of group and who the members of the group are. In the right-hand column we explain what kind of work that group might undertake.

This figure provides an overview of how coaches can group teachers in order to undertake coaching work. Now that we have given a sense of the context and groupings that support that context, we will discuss how coaches might systematically observe.

FIGURE 3.1: Kinds of Grouping and the Work the Groups Can Do

Kind of Grouping	Work That Can Be Undertaken
Whole group	*The coach can* • focus attention of the group • shape concern around what teachers can do • explain how to conduct inquiry • share documentation of teaching • model teaching in a live setting • model teaching using a proxy, such as role play or videotape • assist teachers in evaluating their own teaching *Teachers can* • monitor and evaluate their progress • share challenges • obtain feedback and insights from others • share success
Small group of teachers observes a class taught by a peer	*Observers can* • conference with the teacher prior to observation on challenges in teaching • observe teaching in an authentic setting and take notes • conference with the teacher and each other during the debriefing *The teacher can* • pose questions and solicit assistance in the prebriefing • model innovations the teacher has attempted • share troubling teaching problems in the prebriefing, teaching, and debriefing • pose questions, obtain feedback, and seek future directions for inquiry in the debriefing
Behind a one-way mirror, the coach and a small group of teachers observe a peer teaching a lesson	*The coach can* • guide the observers' observations and analysis of teaching decisions during and after the lesson taught behind the one-way mirror • identify and highlight challenges during the teaching not identified in the prebriefing

	Observers can
	• pose questions aloud during the teaching
	• observe with the assistance of discussion
	• ask clarifying questions of the coach and each other
	• debrief with the assistance of the coach
	The teacher can
	• solicit feedback from and focus the observation of teachers and the coach in the prebriefing
	• benefit from the enhanced observation of teachers who can talk aloud during the observation
	• potentially have both teaching and observation taped in the lablike setting
One teacher observes a peer being coached	*Teacher, coach, and observer can*
	• talk on a teacher-to-teacher level
	• share common concerns regarding teaching and coaching
	• focus more exclusively on the concerns of the observer and the teacher
	• observe the class with the least interruption from outsiders, possibly yielding the most authentic representation of classroom life
Teachers who work with the same students during the school day (e.g., the ESL teacher and the classroom teacher) observe each other teach	*Both teachers can*
	• observe the same students in a different classroom setting
	• learn the nature of the curriculum and instruction being experienced by the student when he or she is in a different classroom
	• learn the concerns of other teachers who are either inside or outside the coaching network
One coach observes one teacher in the coaching network	*Both coach and teacher can*
	• ask the most powerful questions of each other about specific teaching events
	• work toward an understanding of a particular group of students
	• build together a more comprehensive understanding of teaching and learning

CHAPTER 4

Systematic Observation of Teaching

with Carrie Hung

Even though we know that expertise in teaching is clearly related to student progress in school (Block, Oakar, & Hurt, 2002; Darling-Hammond, 1996), there is little research about what it is that effective literacy coaches do to develop that expertise (Dole, 2004). In fact, although coaching has become a key component in the professional development repertoire of many school districts across the United States, we know little about how coaches coach. Joyce and Showers's *Student Achievement Through Staff Development* (1995) is often referenced in this regard, but their work is mostly at the system level; they consider how a district support system for teacher professional development might be designed and make recommendations about the content of those programs. The best evidenced-based descriptions of how coaches coach comes from Lyons and Pinnell (2001) and Lyons (2002). Our goal in this chapter is to add to their work by describing our findings about how coaches observe and analyze teaching.

THE VALUE OF SYSTEMATIC, DIRECT OBSERVATION OF TEACHING

In Chapter 2 we said that learning occurs when individuals change the way they participate in an activity. By this we mean that prior to learning something, individuals might participate in an activity in one way, and after learning something they would participate in a different way. Since these differences are often observable, it makes sense that we should examine the nature of teachers' participation in instructional activities to look for evidence of learning. *Participation* refers to how the learning activity is structured, what the teacher says and does during the activity, and how all these things change over time. For example, coaches can look for changes in the way a guided reading lesson is conducted or for shifts in how content area reading is integrated throughout the day. The most effective way to determine changes in instruction is through direct, systematic observation of the teaching in action.

Why not rely on teacher self-reports of changes in teaching to inform the coaching process? After all, it is time consuming to observe teaching. In addition to the travel time involved, the coach has to sit through a lesson and observe. Wouldn't it be easier and simpler to ask teachers to report what they have been doing differently?

Self-reports are not very reliable. According to Hops, Davis, and Longoria (1995), researchers in the field of clinical psychology began moving away from self-reports in the 1960s in favor of direct observation because it was thought that subjects' reports about their own behavior were likely to be biased and, therefore, unreliable. In some cases, for example, individuals who were asked to provide reports of their behavior focused on negative experiences and ignored positive ones.

Direct observation is also a commonly used research approach in education. It has been used to study teaching since the 1930s, when researchers began to explore teacher-student interactions and other classroom behaviors (Evertson & Green, 1986). Like researchers in clinical psychology, education researchers realized that there can be little doubt about the instructional activities in the classroom when they are directly observed. A teacher's self-report might be influenced by personal bias, perception, and an under- or overestimation of how new instructional practices are taken on (although in our experience we have found that teachers consistently underestimate how well they are doing). In any case, direct observation by a coach likely yields more reliable information about the instructional practices than a teacher's self-reports about how things are going.

The value placed on direct observation in education is evident in the way teachers are assessed by the National Board for Professional Teaching Standards for national board certification. In addition to submitting a portfolio of artifacts that represents their teaching and their reflections on their teaching, applicants provide a collection of teaching videotapes. While portfolios are highly regarded as an effective assessment tool, they still require that an evaluator make inferences from the materials about the teaching. Videotapes, on the other hand, provide evaluators with a way to directly observe teaching. As Hops and colleagues (1995) noted, "Unlike traditional assessment in which a person's score on an instrument represents some level of an underlying, covert trait, little inference from direct observation is required because data are collected on the specific behaviors of interest" (p. 194). The challenge of direct observation, of course, lies in learning how to observe practice in productive ways that will enrich the subsequent feedback and joint inquiry—in other words, becoming an effective coach.

CONTEXT FOR THE STUDY: LITERACY COLLABORATIVE

Lyons and Pinnell (2001) studied coaching practices within the context of Literacy Collaborative, a research-based comprehensive literacy framework to guide reading, writing, phonics, and word-study instruction in K–6 classrooms (see http://www.literacycollaborative.org). In addition to its instructional framework, a central feature of Literacy Collaborative is the ongoing work of a school-based literacy coach, called a literacy coordinator, who works closely with individual teachers to help them create positive learning environments, organize powerful teaching opportunities, and make instructional decisions based upon the needs of individual students, and, with younger students, read books at home using Keep Books (see http://www.keepbooks.org).

This model of professional development and literacy instruction assumes that teachers grow professionally and learn by doing with the continuing support of these school-based coaches, who also teach courses, model lessons, observe classroom teaching, and provide coaching aimed at shifting teaching to a higher level of precision based on students' needs.

Lyons and Pinnell (2001) described literacy coordinators' decision making as analytical and recursive in nature, turning on the coach's systematic observation and analysis of teaching. The coach works from these observations to select powerful coaching points that lead the teacher to deeper conceptual understandings and new learning (Lyons, 2002; Lyons & Pinnell, 2001).

Emily and Carrie, the latter a doctoral student at Ohio State, used this coaching setting to learn more about how effective coaches coach. They used the following two questions to guide their inquiry:

1. How do coaches analyze teaching?
2. What are their understandings of quality teaching?

Exploring these questions will bring us closer to the heart of coaching: the analysis that forms the basis for the coaches' interactions with teachers.

Conducting Study on Rubric Development

Literacy Collaborative coaches were invited to participate in a pilot project to develop observational rubrics. Rubrics are written descriptions of levels of enactment, usually from the least to the most idealized form. Rubrics for essay writing, for example, might include four descriptions: one of a poorly constructed essay, one of a below-average essay, one of an average essay, and one of an ideal essay. A teacher evaluates the student's essay-writing sample by comparing it against the rubric to see which features are present.

Rubrics are useful not only for evaluation purposes, but also for teaching. They communicate the range of kinds of performance to teachers and students, allowing participants to set themselves concrete goals for improvement. Teachers often find writing rubrics a valuable activity because it requires them to think about what an ideal example would look like; it is an even more valuable activity when developed with colleagues.

The observational rubrics for this study were initially developed by a group of faculty involved with coaching coaches for the Literacy Collaborative project. We wrote approximately 60 rubrics to describe general instructional practices and specific teaching practices related to each lesson component. Here is an example of one of three rubrics that we wrote for the lesson component called Interactive Read-Aloud. Notice how each description moves closer to an idealized form:

- Teacher begins read-aloud with limited or no interaction about the book or topic to prepare students as listeners.
- Teacher provides some opportunity for students to think about the book to be read, but the interaction may be unfocused or only marginally related to the book topic.
- Teacher engages in some preliminary interaction about the book that at least partially engages students' attention and prepares them to listen.
- Teacher engages attention of the students prior to reading with brief comments or questions, preparing students for active listening and response.

The long-term goal of our study was to establish the reliability and validity of the observational rubrics. Once developed, these rubrics would eventually be used by the literacy coordinators as a tool for observing teaching and supporting coaching decisions. In this volume, we do not name all the rubrics, because they are specific to the Literacy Collaborative instructional framework; our focus here is to describe what we learned from piloting these observational rubrics about how effective coaches observe and analyze teaching.

The coaches involved with piloting these rubrics received 2 days of training on how to use them. They viewed multiple videotapes of instructional practices from the Literacy Collaborative framework and used the rubrics to observe, analyze, and rate the instruction. (We should mention here that typically we would not advise coaches to rate teaching. Ratings were necessary in this case in order to establish the reliability and validity of the observational rubrics.) Following their observations of each videotape, the coaches compared their ratings with those of others and discussed rationales for why they rated the instruction as they had. Although we continued to collect data for the rest of the year on how the coaches used the observational rubrics, the findings reported in this chapter come from the data that Emily and Carrie collected and analyzed from the initial 2-day training session.

To address the two questions posed earlier about how coaches analyze teaching and what they understand about quality teaching, we transcribed and analyzed their small-group discussions about their ratings of each instructional element. We also collected the rubrics and analyzed the coaches' anecdotal comments, written directly onto the rubrics as they observed the videotapes.

Analyzing the Data on Rubric Development

We used a constant comparative method of data analysis, as informed by Strauss and Corbin (1998), to discern common themes across the coaches' handwritten comments on the rubrics and within the transcriptions of their discussions about their rubric ratings. Each researcher analyzed the data set independently and then both met to discuss and reach agreement on emerging categories and themes. Patton (1990) refers to this kind of data analysis—when two people look at the same data set—as a form of analytical triangulation of data analysis. This independent and shared analysis with multiple passes at the data contributes to the trustworthiness of our analysis.

In our first phase of data analysis we compiled all the handwritten notes that the coaches made on the rubrics while they observed the videotapes. We regarded these handwritten comments as "notes to self" because the coaches were not asked to write anything down while they viewed the videotapes. We assume that the coaches made notes about the kinds of things that they wanted to recall later.

We organized our observations into three categories of comments. We noted that many of the written notes were descriptive in nature, with the coach actually scripting the teachers' talk and the students' responses. We coded these kinds of descriptive comments as *What I Observed*. We searched through the remaining notes to see if the coaches evaluated what they observed and found that although they did, their notes were only about instructional practices that they thought did not go well. None of the comments described what they thought went well. We called this second category of notes *What Went Wrong*. The third category of comment to emerge was *Rubric Reflections,* in which the coaches noted questions or confusions that they had about the content of the rubrics. This last category did not occur as frequently as the first two categories.

With these categories in mind, we began our second phase of analysis. We transcribed the small-group discussions of rubric ratings and then read through the transcripts for themes related to our research questions. We found that the coaches' talk as they compared and discussed their ratings could be grouped around two related themes: teacher decision making and student response.

We then coded the coaches according to those themes. We found that the coaches' analyses of teacher decision making could be categorized in terms of the responsiveness of the teacher's actions and the relevance of the actions. In other words, it seemed that the coaches' analyses revolved around two questions:

1. Do the students need to know this; is it relevant?
2. Is the teacher being responsive to the students?

This data-analysis process led us to the patterns that we describe in the following section, about how coaches observe and analyze teaching as well as what they consider to be quality teaching.

Observing and Analyzing Teaching: Coaches at Work

In response to our first research question, about how coaches analyzed teaching, we found that coaches' observations were almost clinical in nature, often scripting exactly what they were seeing and hearing. Our second research question addressed how coaches analyzed quality teaching. Our analysis of the coaches' discussions about their ratings on the rubrics led us to identify three lenses—or ways of looking—that influenced their observations: the pedagogy lens, the responsiveness lens, and the relevancy lens. We discuss both these findings in depth in the sections that follow.

Systematic Observation. When we compared the coaches' scripted notes on their rubrics, as they watched the videotapes, we were surprised to find that the coaches tended to select the very same teaching interactions to script. Most, for example, transcribed the teacher's introduction to a new book, writing down the vocabulary that the teacher discussed before reading the story. Most also wrote down exactly what the teacher said the story was about. This similarity was interesting to us because even though the coaches observed the lesson at the same time, they recorded their observations independently. There was no way that any of them could know what other coaches were writing.

As we further analyzed the content of the coaches' transcriptions, we noted that coaches tended to script specific teaching points that they did not agree with; in other words, they scripted interactions that they thought did not go well. We inferred that had these been actual coaching sessions, the coaches would have wanted access to a written record of those particular interactions that they perhaps would return to later.

How do we account for the similarities across the coaches' observations? It would not make sense to write down every word that was uttered, yet when they wrote they tended to record the same things. It was as though the coaches were making sense of their observations in much the same way, using a similar filter or lens to sift and sort their observations.

The Pedagogy Lens. Adrian conceptualized a mechanism called a *pedagogical lens* to help understand how the same teaching might be viewed and interpreted differently by different people (A. Rodgers, 2002). A literacy lesson that included explicit instruction in phonics, for example, might be considered timely and instructive by one person but lacking in quality by someone else who thinks that phonics instruction should also be systematic, preplanned, and by necessity decontextualized.

It may be that because of the prevalence of formal schooling, we all—whether we are educators, coaches, parents, or policymakers—have our own pedagogical lens through which we understand and evaluate teaching. What is interesting in this present study is not the variability of the coaches' observations and analyses, but its similarity. The coaches seemed to use a very similar lens through which to view instruction, judging by the commonalities across their scripted observations about how the lesson was going. It's as though they had a shared pedagogical lens that suggested something like, "This is a guided reading lesson, therefore I expect to see . . ."

No doubt the coaches in our study had a similar pedagogy lenses because they had all taken extensive professional development training to be Literacy Collaborative coaches. We suspect that no matter what training or preparation a coach has received to prepare for the role, there will always be this pedagogy lens that will influence their observations and analysis of teaching. In the example that follows, the pedagogy lens is clearly at work in the coach's observations. In other words, it is obvious that the coach is observing and analyzing the teaching in terms of how the teacher should teach word solving.

> I thought she gave a lot of clues. She should have had them attempt the word. She kept pointing to the picture, and one boy looked at her and she said, "Look at the word." She never really did get them to look at any of the sounds; there wasn't any word solving at all. (Sheila, literacy coordinator)

This observation suggests that the coach thought there was undue attention given to using the pictures as clues to identify unfamiliar words in the story; there should have been more instruction in word solving (decoding unfamiliar words), specifically learning more about letter-sound relationships. It seems that the coach's observation of how the teaching was going did not fit with her pedagogical lens or what she expected to see.

The transcripts that follow provide two more examples of coaches from our study. Both coaches are reflecting on the same videotape. The similarity across their observation is evident: both think the teacher should have involved the students more in thinking about the meaning of the story along with the attention to decoding words. One coach said,

> I felt that the students needed to be engaged more in the conversation because a lot of it was more like, "What will you see in *cry*?" or "What does *went* begin like?" [She should have worked] more with the story rather than just parts of what you hear. (Keisha, literacy coordinator)

The coach in this next example, commenting on the same excerpt, also addressed the *how* of teaching in her observation and comes to much the same conclusion:

> In that particular book maybe, if she maybe alluded to why the boy became the lamb's mother and not other animals'. It's just like going beyond the literal a little bit—maybe just not really having a full-blown discussion, but still alluding to the fact that there is a turn of events here, what would be the rationale for it, let's find out about it. She got them engaged in the text, but not to anticipating the deeper thinking. (Jackie, literacy coordinator)

In our discussion thus far of how the literacy coaches in our study observed teaching, we have described what we call the pedagogy lens; that is, the coaches seemed to take into account the *how* of teaching. In a way, this measure is similar to a test of face validity. It's as though the coaches asked themselves, "Does this look like what I'd expect this particular component (teaching for fluency, word solving, comprehension, etc.) to look like?" Another way of summarizing this kind of analysis would be to say, "Yes, that looks like a guided reading lesson" or "That's not the way a book introduction should go."

The Responsiveness Lens. When the coaches in our study discussed rationales for their ratings, they often referred to what we call the responsiveness of teaching as a factor in their analysis. For example, coaches cited a lack of teacher responsiveness to how students were learning as a rationale for giving a low rating to a video segment of instruction. By *lack of responsiveness* the coaches meant that the teacher seemed to be following a set agenda without noticing whether the teaching was too easy or too hard for the students. One coach summed up the *responsiveness lens* nicely when she said, "What you're really looking for is, is she meeting the needs of those kids?"

Another coach had this to say about a lesson, after giving the book introduction a low rating on the observational rubric. Notice her comment that the teacher was not being responsive to the students, but instead was teaching in a routine way:

> I was thinking that her introduction was a bit lengthy; she gave the whole story away. I don't think she did it because they needed it. Maybe it was just something she usually did and she just got on a roll. (Kiearra, literacy coordinator)

Another coach in the same small discussion group agreed with that observation, saying,

> I kind of agree. I thought there must be some students there who were learning to speak English, and that's why the teacher was being so supportive with labels, concepts, and vocabulary in the story she was introducing. So I thought maybe it's an appropriate level after all. (Gail, literacy coordinator)

In fact, the responsiveness lens played such a large role in the coaches' observations and analysis of teaching that they often formed hypotheses like the one in the previous example to explain the mismatch between the teaching they were observing and what they thought the students could do. Another coach, commenting on the same videotape of teaching, said,

> I felt that her book introduction was too heavy; she gave so, so much support in order for the kids to take on the reading, I thought maybe it could be the first time they read that level so

you always would want to give a higher amount of support at
the beginning. . . . I just felt like the book introduction was very
lengthy so I was concerned about the text selection. It was too
hard for them. (Gabriella, literacy coordinator)

Clearly the coaches in our study were taking into account the degree of
responsiveness present in the teaching. They expected teaching to be
matched to how students were responding and what they were able to do.
The coaches noted whether they thought a teacher was doing something
that the student already knew how to do, or couldn't do even with help,
and this factor played into their analysis of the teaching.

The Relevancy Lens. A third dimension of coaches' observations had
to do with the relevancy of teaching—what we refer to as the *relevancy
lens*. Their reflections on their ratings also dealt with whether they thought
students could profit from the teaching; this could only happen if what
the teacher was teaching matched what students could use to learn. One
coach, for example, made the following comment when sharing her rationale for her rubric rating:

The teacher said, "You did what good readers do, you went back
and fixed it," but she really didn't go back into the text and say,
"This is what you did." The student went all the way back here
and reread. I'm not sure he made the connection about what the
teacher meant: to go back and reread. (Sonya, literacy coordinator)

According to the coach's analysis, the teacher's comment was likely
not relevant to the student, because the student did not know what the
teacher was referring to in her comment. The teacher wasn't really teaching exactly what it was the student needed to know. In other words, the
coach analyzed a gap between what the teacher was doing and what the
student could use. Specifically, the coach thought that the teacher's comment "You went back and fixed it" was probably too vague to be useful
and relevant for the student at this time. More specific teaching was needed. The teacher might have said something like, "Good job checking on
yourself when you fixed up that word [perhaps pointing to the wrongly
read word]. Were you right?" If the coach was correct that the student
needed more specific teaching at this point to know what "went back and
fixed it" meant, then this alternative teaching might be more relevant and
useful to the student.

Another coach, reflecting on a different videotape, gave the following
rationale for her rubric rating. Note how the relevancy lens comes into

play as the coach describes how she analyzed the teaching:

> She just let things happen which I know that's good to do, but she didn't have a focus. The word *random* came to mind. By bringing the student up to the chart paper, she needed to have a teaching point. But instead she just got into talking about how the student didn't have any front teeth. So there was no teaching, even though she could have said something that she [the student] was doing well and make some teaching from that. (Marjorie, literacy coordinator)

In this example, we can see how relevancy plays a role in the coach's observation of the teaching interaction. The coach expects the teacher to really teach, questions teaching moves that are not meaningful or useful for the students, and notes missed opportunities for learning.

CONCLUSION

We began this chapter by pointing out that there is very little research on what it is that effective literacy coaches do (Dole, 2004). We had a unique opportunity in this study to gain insight into this very question by having coaches view and rate teaching videotapes, and then share and discuss their ratings in small groups. Again, we point out that while we believe that coaching teachers is not about rating their teaching performance, the way coaches rated teaching in this study helped us understand how they interpreted teaching. The coaches' rating of teachers that we report here is not what we recommend that coaches do; rather, the rating represents a research tool that can help us better understand what coaches do when they observe teaching.

The coaches in this study were not following a manual or checklist to tell them what teachers ought to be saying or doing at particular times throughout a lesson. Instead, the coaches observed teaching in a systematic way, even going so far as to script specific teaching interactions. We were interested in how they decided what to script and how we could account for the similarities in their teacher ratings.

Our analysis of the coaches' discussion following their analysis led us to conceptualize three lenses through which they viewed the teaching. The pedagogy lens filtered their observations of how the teaching was going. The responsiveness and relevancy lenses led them to judge whether the teaching was relevant to the children's needs and whether it was pitched at an appropriate level.

It was interesting to note that even though the coaches were observing teaching, their focus was not limited to the teacher and what the teacher was saying and doing. Instead, their observations included the students in terms of how they were responding and participating in the lesson. We might say that the coaches' way in to analyzing the teaching was through the students. The coaches noted whether the students were about to profit from the instruction, whether the teacher was keeping it easy enough for the students to learn, and whether the focus of the teaching was what students needed to learn at that particular time. As Lyons (2002) suggests, "Coaching should never focus on what the teacher is doing right or wrong, but how the students are learning as a result of teaching" (p. 96).

The coach's lenses used to observe and analyze teaching remind us of Wood and Wood's (1996) description of the nature of scaffolding. He said that teaching decisions take into account when to teach, what to teach, and how to teach and that these decisions are often made on a moment-by-moment basis as the teacher decides what to say or what to do next. The *what* and *how* to teach are informed by knowledge of the subject matter and knowledge about how to teach. The *when* decision, according to Wood, is probably the most difficult to make because it requires the teacher to match the content to the student. We are not referring here to the larger curriculum-related decisions about what material to cover when during the year, but the moment-by-moment decisions teachers make about when students are ready for a new concept or a new procedure. This decision is informed by the student's participation and can be summed up by the questions, Have I prepared my students to learn like this? and Will I introduce this concept now?

Similarly the coach's lenses filter their observations to consider the *how* (pedagogy), the *what* (relevance), and the *when* (responsiveness) of teaching. It is as though the dimension of scaffolding became the yardstick that guides coaches' observations and led them to distinguish quality teaching from less-than-quality teaching. This is an extremely significant finding.

One thing seems certain. Coaches need to be well prepared in the subject matter so they can observe teaching in terms of the *what*, *how*, and *when* kinds of discussions that teachers need to make. No doubt a coach with minimal training can observe teaching in terms of *what* is being taught. This is particularly true, and no doubt particularly easy, if the teachers are following a set curriculum that mandates what should be taught and when. In that case, coaching can be reduced to observing with a checklist to see if particular components are being taught as specified by the core curriculum. Does the teacher include a lesson on word solving? Does the teacher provide the specified amount of time for familiar rereading? We wouldn't call this teaching, though, nor would we call it coaching.

Teachers need a theoretical understanding of what and how they're teaching in order to be able to make teaching decisions in the moment. As Lyons et al. (1993) noted, without theoretical understandings "lists of good teaching behaviors performed in mechanical ways in response to supervisor's observations, are useless" (p. 43). Recently we were reading an account of coaching, and it struck us as hopeful but also naive:

> One teacher wrote in a reflection "I was really nervous about demonstrating a guided reading lesson for a colleague and then coaching her through similar lessons. We co-planned the lessons and discussed our experiences after each lesson. We both felt that this process was very helpful. I am convinced that this approach will make a positive impact in our school." (Shaw, Smith, Chesler, & Romeo, 2005, p. 10)

We admire the positive attitude and the dedication implicit in this observation, but our experience tells us that coaching is both delicate and sophisticated work. We need more than good intentions, more than a readiness to work hard, and more than a willingness to take risks. In place of this naive assertion, we conclude that coaches need not only knowledge of what should be taught, but also a theory of literacy and learning and an understanding of effective teaching.

NOTE

The work in this chapter was supported by a grant from the Institute for Educational Sciences, R305M040086, "Can Literacy Professional Development be Improved with Web-Based Collaborative Learning Tools: A Randomized Field Trial." All errors of fact, omission, or interpretation are solely the responsibility of the authors.

CHAPTER 5

Scaffolding Reflection

Adrian's brother Randy, a teacher with 30 years' experience, visited us for a week last summer before the start of the new school year. While he was with us, he spent a few hours each day reviewing the new science textbook that he would use in the fall and planning instruction for his fifth-grade class. As he studied the new materials, Randy reflected on his knowledge of fifth-grade students: their background knowledge, their reading levels, and their interests. He considered the curriculum and thought about how the concepts in the new science textbook might be integrated across other subjects throughout the day. Randy also identified sections within the textbook that would likely be difficult for his students to comprehend, and he considered what he might do to support their understanding.

Randy's planning provides a case example of a reflective practitioner at work. As an experienced fifth-grade teacher, Randy has an in-depth knowledge of the curriculum and of students at that grade level. This knowledge and experience, however, is not what makes him an effective teacher; instead it is his ability to reflect on and use this information to plan instruction that will support his teaching.

Clearly the development of reflection is an integral component of initial and ongoing teacher preparation and of a teacher's craft. As Evertson and Green (1986) concluded, when it comes to coaching, the end goal of educational change may be defined as the extent to which teachers reflect on their work.

We have learned, however, that reflecting on practice alone is not enough to make for powerful teaching. A teacher may be able to identify powerful features of teaching practice as well as features that might be changed to create more powerful student learning; but if the teacher lacks the ability, interest, or even time to act on these insights, reflection by itself is not as powerful as it otherwise might be.

Reflection, defined as a careful self-analysis of one's own work, offers much promise as a tool to improve teacher practice because it is integrally connected to teachers' work, as we explain in the first section below. In the sections that follow, we provide a rationale for coaching teacher reflection, identify factors that might get in the way of a teacher's ability to reflect on practice, and offer suggestions for how coaches might provide opportunities within their coaching conversations to promote and support teacher self-reflection.

THE PROMISE OF REFLECTION

Schön (1983) first identified the fact that individuals in multiple professions, including education, use reflection to improve their practice. In an effort to help educators capitalize on these possibilities, Zeichner and Liston (1996) borrowed from Dewey (1944, 1960) to create an operational definition of reflective teaching, saying it was

> an active desire to listen to more sides than one, to give full attention to alternative possibilities, and to recognize the possibility of error even in beliefs that are dearest to us. Teachers who are open-minded are continually examining the rationales that underlie what is taken as natural and right, and take pains to seek out conflicting evidence. (p. 10)

In the same year Sprinthall, Reiman, and Thies-Sprinthall (1996) also borrowed from Dewey to describe reflective action as an "active, persistent and careful consideration of any belief" (p. 688). In both these descriptions of reflection, contemporary educators have chosen to stress active consideration as a principal task of the teacher.

We can deduce from these descriptions that what Dewey called *deliberation* is a very important part of reflective practice. In fact, we might even say that one possibility that might be realized from reflection is that teachers are freed from assumptions so that they might carefully consider their work. As Richardson (1996) explained, "The goal of research in the critical tradition is emancipation through self-reflection, specifically reflection on the underlying assumptions that drive the system in which one operates" (p. 114). Thus we can conclude that reflective practice necessitates:

- Questioning assumptions
- Identifying alternatives
- Weighing options
- Deliberating on how to proceed
- Choosing courses of action
- Planning how to proceed
- Implementing one's plan

We will revisit these components later in the chapter as we discuss formats that support reflection on teaching.

INTEGRATING REFLECTION INTO COACHING PRACTICES:
A RATIONALE

Shulman's (1986) model of pedagogical reasoning describes the steps that teachers take in preparing and teaching a lesson, and within his model we find both an important role for teacher reflection and a context for coaching. The steps include comprehension, transformation, instruction, evaluation, reflection, and new comprehension.

Before a teacher begins planning, there must be *comprehension* of the material. With this initial comprehension, Shulman said, a teacher goes about the process of transforming the material from a text (typically, although not always, a textbook) into something that can be instructed. This *transformation* is a complex task, and it was just the kind of work that Randy was doing when he spent that week of his summer vacation with us. Teachers first prepare by analyzing and segmenting the texts. They must then consider the metaphors, analogies, examples, or demonstrations that might represent the material to students.

After comprehending the task and then considering how to transform it, teachers select what is appropriate from an instructional repertoire of teaching techniques to instruct. *Instruction* requires the teacher to consider how the class, the presentation, and the material will be managed. In the *evaluation* stage, teachers evaluate both the teaching and the student response to the teaching.

Finally the teacher *reflects* on the whole experience thus far. Reflection can actually change the way the teacher conceived of the teaching along each stage of the process, from comprehending through transforming, teaching, and then evaluation. It allows the teacher to undertake *new comprehensions* of new material to come, or new students to teach, or recomprehensions of one's whole way of teaching.

Shulman (1986) contended that this rich realm of different kinds of teacher knowledge offers great opportunities for coaching teacher change. If teachers are engaged in the process of thinking about what they will teach and how, they will need much more than subject content knowledge alone; they also need pedagogical content knowledge. This is a different kind of knowledge in that teachers integrate what they know about the content with what they know about how to teach that content in a particular context.

Shulman's (1986) pedagogical model is very useful because it suggests that reflection is an integral part of teaching as opposed to an extra or a frill. Literacy coaches can build upon the reflection that teachers already go through rather than ask busy teachers to undertake an extra task. Perhaps most important, Shulman's model provides a context within which to situate the literacy coach's work. By guiding teacher reflection about what was taught and how, the literacy coach can support the teacher in new comprehensions about instruction along each phase within the model. It is in this last phase that literacy coaches may be able to take the reflections of teachers and support them in developing new possibilities as to how they might teach their students.

Randy, whom we introduced at the beginning of this chapter, had already started the process of comprehending the material and transforming it to suit the needs of his students. We can imagine that if a coach were present to support his subsequent reflection on the teaching of that material, that coach would have had a rich and in-depth analysis, because Randy had already given much thought to the process and would have developed new comprehensions about instruction and even recomprehensions about his teaching.

A final rationale for coaching teacher reflection is that it is the kind of work that lends itself to exploration through conversation; reflection, therefore, fits hand in glove with the coaching process. Not only is the match between reflection and conversation a natural fit, it opens new opportunities to support the coaching process. According to Sprinthall et al. (1996), Schön argued that the "dialogue between coach and student in a reflective practicum is . . . a needed exemplar for a new epistemology of practice" (p. 689).

Fullan (1991) offered a helpful synopsis of the historic research on collaborative forms of professional development, including reflection. After examining a number of studies that focused on teacher change by considering how teachers could rethink "what they teach and how they teach it" (p. 55), he concluded that

- Teachers engaged in frequent, continuous, and increasingly concrete talk about teaching practice
- Teachers and administrators . . . develop[ed] a shared language for teaching strategies and needs
- Teachers and administrators planned, designed, and evaluated teaching materials and practices together

When we use these same concepts and apply them to a coaching context, we can see that especially with regard to reflection, there is the promise that reflection offers an opportunity for teachers to

- Talk in concrete terms about what they do now and what they could do in the future
- Develop shared ownership and language and, therefore, shared understanding
- Share the work of changing teaching practices through coaching

Now that we have established a rationale for coaching teacher reflection, we will turn to a discussion of its limitations. With those cautions in mind, we then discuss ways that coaches can provide opportunities to promote and support teacher self-reflection.

LIMITATIONS OF REFLECTION

Although reflection is a powerful tool, educators must be wary about over-promising what might be realized. It is tempting to believe (or even hope) that simply through careful deliberation on teaching practices we might change our teaching overnight, but this is not the case, because of two sets of factors. The first is that there are many forces beyond our control as teachers; they interfere with what changes we would like to make in our teaching and what changes we can actually realize. The second has to do with our own choices as teachers and our own feelings about what is important.

Interference Posed by External Factors

One promise offered by reflection is that teachers might be able to free themselves of assumptions about their students or their instruction. While this may be true, the degree to which teachers can act on this insight is limited by the school culture in which a teacher works.

Recently we were talking with some teachers about a literacy program adopted by their school district. Instead of selecting one program, the district decided to develop its own by borrowing features from a number of programs. As a result, the district's core literacy program became a hodge-podge of programs that were highly scripted, without an evidence base, and composed of what the teachers viewed as redundant tasks that took them away from teaching. When the teachers were asked how such a program came to be implemented, they said that the decision had been calculated to encounter the least resistance from what had become a highly politicized debate about which literacy program the district would adopt. The teachers also explained that their adherence to key features of the program was monitored by district-level inspectors who scolded teachers for deviations from the published scripts.

What we take from this particular case is that both coaches and teachers often find themselves in politicized contexts in which adherence to particular teaching practices is the order of the day. In such contexts, reflection can become almost depressing, since one initially thinks of all the possible changes one can make to teaching, but then recognizes the barriers to those changes.

Yet no matter the instructional context, there will be boundaries to changes in practice. Even within very prescriptive contexts, coaches and teachers can still work together to reflect on teaching. We suggest, therefore, that coaches and teachers not throw the reflective baby out with the contextual bathwater and work together on teaching within whatever boundaries exist.

Interference Posed by Internal Factors

Placing an emphasis on reflection within the coaching context assumes that teachers are willing and able to reflect on their teaching practices and take action to recomprehend their teaching. While we think that this is true of most teachers, certainly it may not be true of every teacher who is being coached. Reflection on teaching practice is an intensely personal process. When prompted to reflect, it is certainly understandable that teachers may have a focus different from that of the coach. Indeed, in reflecting on their teaching, teachers may spend quite a lot of time reflecting on factors beyond their control, whereas coaches may want teachers to focus on aspects of teaching that are within their control.

The answer to resolving this dual focus lies in the ability of coaches and teachers to negotiate the reflective process. As one coach recently told us, "In my own coaching I used to think of what is most advantageous to the teacher. It was what I thought she needed, but I am not sure if it was what the teacher thought she needed." Thus reflection is more than an opportunity to have teachers reflect on their teaching. The coach should also be reflective. Reflection, then, is an opportunity for coaches and teachers to think together about the teaching and what is to come out of the reflective process. It is not helpful to the process if coaches have such ownership over the reflection that the teachers' voices are silenced. Through joint reflection, co-ownership of the coaching process can be built.

A second internal factor that might get in the way of using reflection as a tool for coaching is the teacher's capacity to move from observation to a real change in teaching practices. Although this may seem an obvious step, taking it is anything but easy. While we may be able to articulate the need for change, it is not easy to change teaching practices that have become inured over time. For example, despite the fact that many of us may want to lose weight and we know the strategies that will help us achieve that goal, it is extremely difficult for most people to make the obvious lifestyle changes required. Just as our relationship with food, exercise, and weight is an intensely personal one, so too is our relationship with teaching. It may be just as challenging to go from reflection and an understanding about how teaching should or could change to actually changing.

SCAFFOLDING REFLECTION TO FOSTER CHANGE

Although most teachers are quite accomplished in their teaching, we think that the job of the coach is to work with teachers at the edge of their learning. In other words, if a teacher is a novice the coach may be working at some rather basic teaching techniques. When working with a more experienced teacher, a coach may be working at both their own and the teacher's edge of expertise as they problem-solve together. Thus we have found Wood, Bruner, and Ross's (1976) term *scaffolding* to be helpful in describing the coaching process because it emphasizes supporting learning at the edge of one's learning (see A. Rodgers & E. Rodgers, 2004). To undertake this work a coach will likely pose some questions with a teacher or teachers, prior to starting their work, that are calculated to get at teaching goals. This might include such questions as, "Can you tell me three things that you are working on in your teaching?" or "What are three things that you plan to change in your teaching that we will look for next time?" By undertaking this work, the coach can support teachers in initiating inquiry.

Side Coaching: Reflection-in-Action

In this section we focus on techniques that can promote reflection in settings where a teacher and coach are working together one to one, or in group settings where teachers are talking with each other and their coach. As we discuss the techniques, we will link them to Schön's (1983) concepts of *reflection-on-action* and *reflection-in-action*. Reflection-on-action occurs after teaching has been completed, while reflection-in-action occurs within the moment-by-moment analysis that teachers undertake to determine the next choice regarding instruction.

Reflection-in-action occurs in the head of the teacher and, therefore, does not lend itself to examination. Occasionally a coach observing teaching might catch the teacher pausing ever so briefly as if deliberating on the next move. Although reflection-in-action is almost invisible, it is at the moment of deliberation that we propose that a coach could *side coach*.

Many of us who have been coached outside the teaching context have encountered side coaching. Side coaching supports reflection-in-action. It occurs when the coach provides directions during the performance. If you are the third trombone player in an orchestra and the conductor cues your entrance during a performance, you have received side coaching. If the hockey coach yells, "Pass the puck!" and you do, you have been side coached. It is likely that these actions have been discussed prior to the performance or game, so that the person being coached understands the direction and knows how to act on it. We can see from these examples that side coaching

- Is intended to support a fledgling behavior that is the focus of the coaching
- Occurs during a performance
- Must be extremely explicit and highly directed

If the person being coached knows how to use the direction and the coaching is provided at an optimal time during the performance (just when it is needed), side coaching can result in a superior performance.

Likewise, literacy coaches attempting side coaching would likely only do so based on prior conferencing when the teacher has asked for a very specific kind of help and is expecting the coach to intervene during the teaching with a brief direction. Thus side coaching is a way of reinforcing and providing guidance to support reflection-in-action that is informed by previous discussions between and analyses by the coach and teacher. Some researchers have attempted more sophisticated side-coaching arrangements using in-ear headsets (Giebelhaus, 1994) with some success, but we contend that this work is not likely to be successful, since side coaching requires such a high degree of specificity that it must be limited to directions of two or three words.

Using Visits to Promote Reflection-on-Action

Unlike reflection-in-action, reflection-on-action is much easier to contrive, mold, and document. Because reflection-on-action takes place after teaching, the coach and teacher do not have to fear interrupting the teaching, and participants can dwell on what they want. In this section we are going to describe formats that support reflection-on-action.

Cluster Visits. At the beginning of this chapter we listed some necessities of reflective practice. The *cluster visits* we describe in this section can support reflective practice because the group approach allows more than one person to question assumptions, choose courses of action, and implement possible plans. Cluster visits occur when a coach is joined by several other teachers who are also being coached on a school visit to another teacher. It is possible that the teacher may feel under undue scrutiny with so many pairs of eyes observing the teaching. The coach will need to work against this natural tendency and instead direct the teachers' focus on the teaching and learning of all teachers attending the session rather than on the one teacher's teaching of a student. One way to do this is to suspend the teaching after a short interval and reflect as a group. Certainly such a technique could work in a classroom that uses a center approach or group work, since students could engage in these activities while the teachers reflected on the teaching. In this kind of circumstance, teachers have the opportunity to almost reflect-in-action by pausing shortly after teaching was undertaken, conduct discussion, and resume teaching. Reflection-on-action can then take place after the entire lesson is complete.

Targeted School Visit. In the *targeted school visit* the coach has selected a particular classroom, classroom teacher, and group of observer-teachers for the purpose of conducting observation and reflection focused around a particular task. For example, if a group of teachers are struggling with introducing a new book to students, the coach may ask that the group attend a classroom where the teacher is particularly adept at introducing the new book. In other cases, perhaps the coach will select a teacher who is struggling with introducing the new book and ask that that teacher host a group of teachers who are adept at introducing new books. In this case, the less-accomplished teacher can model the book introduction and then seek the expert commentary of a number of teachers. The weaker teacher also has the option to ask the more accomplished teachers to model new book introductions by teaching the students. In either of these options, teachers have the ability to reflect on their work, observe additional performances, and then reflect again.

The targeted school visit supports reflective practice because the teachers who are gathered together have a special interest. For example, teachers interested in helping students who have fallen behind their peers may gather together to investigate teaching approaches. In another targeted school-visit scenario, a teacher may lay out a hypothesis to the group about why the student has fallen behind. Prior to observing the teaching, the teachers may sit and ask questions that are meant to get at student learning. They may ask, "What about the choice of book?" or "What about the topic of the book?" In these cases the questions that the observer-teachers ask are not meant to solve problems; rather, they serve to probe teacher beliefs and instructional possibilities. At this same time alternative hypotheses can be explored as a springboard to teaching and careful observation of the student. After this work is completed the coach may say, "Let's get the student in here and observe what happens." Following 10 minutes of observation the coach and teachers may stop to debrief. After this work the coach might suggest that the teacher try a different hypothesis, bring the student back in, and teach again.

Rolling Cluster Visit. A sequence of individual classroom visits coupled with cluster visits is called a *rolling cluster visit*. For example, in the first week a coach might undertake individual visits to Teachers A, B, C, and D. Within a few weeks the coach and Teachers A, B, and C might all go to visit Teacher D at the same time. A couple of weeks after that the coach and Teachers B, C, and D might visit Teacher A; and a couple of weeks after that the coach and Teachers C, D, and A might visit Teacher B. There is also the possibility that during this sequence a coach might continue individual classroom visits.

At the beginning of the rolling cluster visit, the coach might begin with an individual classroom visit to one or more teachers for the purpose of laying important groundwork. The cluster visit builds on this work and in turn feeds back to individual classroom visits. After the initial round of visits, the coach can start looking for evidence of changed teaching practices based on the preceding work. A way to gain additional power from the rolling cluster visit is to have multiple groups of teachers in different schools working at the same time.

Colleague Visits. Similar to cluster visits are *colleague visits*, except they occur without the presence of the coach. When a small group of teachers visits one teacher, there is the opportunity to undertake reflective practice by questioning assumptions, choosing courses of action, and implementing possible plans. What is significant about working without the coach is that a more authentic school context—in which teachers work with another teacher but outside the coaching context—is approximated.

Targeted Coaching. According to several authors (Joyce & Showers, 1988; Thies-Sprinthall in Phillips & Glickman, 1991) it may take as long as 50 hours to 6 months for a teacher to change the way he or she teaches. Targeted coaching is based on an educational model in which the coach and teacher agree to work together especially closely and intensely on specific components of teaching. The goal is to support the teacher so that change in instructional practices does not take 50 hours to 6 months, but can occur at a much quicker pace.

To get started on this intensive work, we suggest two techniques. One is the *focused coaching protocol*, which emphasizes cycles of observation and debriefing, and the other is the *videotape protocol*, which involves guided analysis of videotaped samples of teaching.

In focused coaching the coach observes a teacher teach a short lesson, about 10 minutes long. This excerpt is selected because it permits the observation of the kinds of teaching of interest to the coach and the teacher. After the 10-minute increment the teacher and coach stop, reflect, and discuss. On the basis of this work the teacher teaches again for another 10-minute increment or so. The nature of the second teaching increment depends on a lot of things. Perhaps it is a reteaching in an effort to enhance the teaching strategy. In other cases the teacher might use a different teaching strategy based on the coaching conversation. In still other cases the coach and teacher may test a different educational hypothesis.

A second technique that could be used at a different time or with a different teacher is a *videotape protocol*. In this scenario a coach might ask a teacher to make multiple videotapes of teaching using a particular strategy. For example, a teacher might videotape three new book introductions. The coach and teacher could then reflect on these videotapes together. The coach's presence acts to focus the reflection of the teacher. The collaborators can then create a plan for future action, and the session might conclude with a live lesson taught by the teacher and featuring side coaching by the coach.

In suggesting these two techniques we can see that there is the opportunity for teachers to reflect on their work and then hone their teaching using rehearsal strategies. As Thies-Sprinthall (in Phillips & Glickman, 1991) noted, reflection is an essential tool for developing teacher thinking; it includes individual analysis and joint debriefing, an ongoing cycle of teaching and reflecting, close collaboration between the coach and the coached, and an acknowledgment of the process of reflection and collaboration through the need to undertake a sustained commitment to coaching and developing teaching lasting several months.

CONCLUSION

For many years educational researchers working with both pre- and inservice teachers have relied on reflection as a construct that has held great promise for changing teaching practices. While it is true that reflection is a powerful tool, literacy coaches must be wary of its limitations. It is critical that coaches seek opportunities whereby reflection can provide feed-forward in terms of informing teacher decision making. As one beginning coach told us, "My primary style of teaching was telling. I need to build an understanding with the teachers and share in their analysis. My goal is to get shifts in the teaching and formulate conclusions together." To support this feed-forward process, it is essential that coaches scaffold teachers at the point of difficulty, adjusting their support in such a way that teachers can use their insights from reflection-in-action and reflection-on-action to enhance teaching. A coach with whom we were working explained that "what became clearer to me was the role of active construction on one's learning and how critical this is in our leading a school visit. Scaffolding the teacher through genuine conversation and questioning will prove to be most productive and generative." We will consider scaffolding teaching more carefully in the following chapter.

CHAPTER 6

Scaffolding Teaching

Scaffolding has been defined as providing help so that a learner can complete a task that would otherwise be beyond his or her unassisted efforts (Wood, Bruner, & Ross, 1976). It sounds simple, yet anyone who has continued to hold on to the back of a child's bike long after the child needed help with balancing (even with the child providing feedback by shouting, "I can do it myself!") has an inkling that scaffolding learning is a complex business (E. Rodgers & A. Rodgers, 2004). How do you know whether and when to withdraw or offer more help? What kind of help do you offer and does it matter?

In this chapter, we draw from research to describe some essential features of scaffolding, and we apply these features to coaches working with literacy teachers. We begin with a definition of learning from a Vygotskian perspective and use the Wood et al. (1976) theory of scaffolding to discuss how literacy coaches can think about the nature of the help they provide to teachers.

LEARNING FOR COACHES

Vygotsky (1978) defined learning as changing participation in an activity. A ski instructor, for example, can tell that a student is learning by noting how the student's participation in skiing changes: shifting direction was a challenge last week; the baby hill was conquered this week; the steeper slope will be tried next week. From this perspective, then, it's important that the teacher observe the learner's participation in an activity in order to plan instruction that is responsive to what the learner is just able to accomplish with some help. This is what is meant by teaching on a learner's cutting edge, or teaching within the learner's *zone of proximal development*.

We do this close observation of participation in an activity more often than you might think. Caregivers, for example, can describe in precise detail what a child can do on any given day in terms of rolling over, standing, or taking a first step; and they can identify daily progress. Teachers also closely observe students' participation in school activities for signs of learning and to help plan instruction. For example, if we observe that a child does not reread when faced with difficulty but simply stops and waits for help, we might teach the child how to search for more information. We would then observe subsequent readings to see if the child's actions changed the next time an unfamiliar word was encountered.

Vygotsky's (1978) perspective has a number of implications for literacy coaching. It is especially helpful in providing guidance to coaches who want to know whether they are having an impact on instructional practices, teacher thinking, and teaching philosophy. It's difficult, after all, for a coach to know whether working with a teacher has brought about deep, lasting, and fundamental change. One coach told us she looked to the teacher's response as a way to measure her impact. "When the teacher gets really enthusiastic about what I'm saying and comes back to me wanting to know more, then I know I've made a difference." But has she really?

As we cited in Chapter 2, David Cohen's (1990) now-classic essay about Mrs. Oublier, a math teacher who enthusiastically incorporated new activities into her math instruction without ever really shifting her thinking about the value of exploration over accuracy, suggests that we might be misled if we relied on teacher response as an indicator of change and learning. For example, a teacher may embrace a different way of interacting with students in introducing new storybooks to young children without really shifting what he or she emphasizes or expects from students during the introduction of the books. How can a coach know if there's been meaningful change in practice and thinking?

Vygostky's (1978) perspective on learning guides us to look at teacher participation in activities as a measure of change. What does the teacher actually say and do when introducing a new storybook to children? What does the teacher attend to or ignore during the introduction? What does the teacher emphasize today that was ignored in the past?

This emphasis on activity means that the coach will need to observe practice, whether taped or in person. In Chapter 4 we offered some specific strategies to systematically observe teaching, but for now, it's just important to note that the goal of observations in this context is not an evaluative one but a necessary step in understanding how the teacher currently participates in an activity. Only then will the coach be able to note changes in the way the teacher participates in the activity and be able to plan support that will scaffold the teacher's understandings.

SCAFFOLDING LEARNING: THE KIND OF HELP MATTERS

It would be easy to scaffold learning if it only involved offering everyone the same kind of help at the same time, disregarding each person's present abilities and understandings or his or her response to the support. Many learning situations are certainly structured that way: University undergraduate classes are offered in a lecture hall and teachers' workshops featuring one presenter are offered to hundreds of attendees. On the other hand, just having one-to-one help doesn't guarantee success either. Computer technical support offered over the telephone is always on a one-to-one basis, but the caller can still experience a great deal of frustration following instructions to solve a computer problem.

In fact, one thing that we have learned from the past 30 years of research on scaffolding is that simply offering help may not do; there seems to be something about the nature of the interactions that contributes to the success of learning (E. Rodgers, 2004). Research suggests that the level of assistance provided to the learner is critical in scaffolding, or lifting, development. Let's consider one of the earliest studies on scaffolding, in which parents worked individually with their children to teach them how to put together a toy pyramid made of interlocking blocks of complex sizes and shapes (Wood & Middleton, 1975). While this context is different from that of coaches working with teachers, the results do inform us about the nature of scaffolding performance. In the Wood and Middleton study, the researchers noted, surprisingly perhaps, that the frequency of help provided didn't necessarily correlate with success. In fact, a child whose mother intervened only 10 times was more successful than a child whose mother intervened 78 times.

It seems, then, that instead of the amount of help, an essential feature of effective scaffolding is pitching help at just the right level of sensitivity. Children whose parents were able to vary the amount of help they offered in response to their child's attempts seemed to provide just the right kind of help needed.

What kinds of help are there? Wood and Middleton (1975) observed five levels in their study (see Figure 6.1).

FIGURE 6.1: Five Levels of Intervention

Intervention	Example
General verbal instruction	"That was good." "Can you make another like that?"
Specific verbal instruction	"Can you find a large one now?"
Indicating what is needed next	"You need that one over there."
Providing material and preparing it	Child has only one step to finish.
Demonstrating what needs to be done	Child does not have to do anything.

Source: Wood & Middleton, 1975

FIGURE 6.2: Teacher Scaffolding Actions from Least to Most Supportive

Category	Definition	Examples
QUESTIONING	The teacher asks the student a question.	"Are you right?" "Does it say *leopard* or *lady?*"
DIRECTING	The teacher directs the student to take a specific action.	"Check it to make sure you're right." "Use the first letter and read that again."
DEMONSTRATING	The teacher takes the student's role and demonstrates a problem-solving action.	The teacher rereads. The teacher articulates the first sound of a word.
TELLING	The teacher tells the student.	"That word is *girl.*"

In Figure 6.1, the levels of help are ordered from least amount of help (a general instruction) to most help (taking the child's part and showing what has to be done). The most disastrous approach, Wood and Middleton (1975) found, was continually offering the most amount of help: just telling or demonstrating for the child how to put the toy together. They concluded that parents who relied on simply modeling the task seemed to convince their children that the task was beyond their ability, and the children eventually lost interest in the project. By contrast, parents who varied their responses by giving less support when their children met with success and more support when difficulty was encountered were able to teach their children how to build the toy independently.

In more recent studies on scaffolding, the focus has moved from parent-child dyads to educational settings with teachers working with students. E. Rodgers (2000b) and Many (2002) identified similar levels of help present in tutoring settings in schools. E. Rodgers (2004) characterized the nature of teacher help in the Reading Recovery lessons that she observed as being situated on a continuum from least to most help and consisting of these kinds of help: questioning the student, directing the student to something helpful, demonstrating a helpful action, or telling the student the solution (see Figure 6.2).

E. Rodgers (2000b) also found that one child's difficulty learning (in this case, literacy learning) was associated with a teacher's pitching help at too high a level. In that case, the teacher frequently directed the student to take some action (such as "Read that again") or questioned the student

("Did that look right?"), but rarely demonstrated any specific problem-solving actions for the student such as rereading or looking at the parts of unfamiliar words.

The point that we can take away from these studies that examined scaffolding children's learning has to do with the nature of help. It's not that any one kind of help is bad and to be avoided, but that the coach should calibrate the kind of help offered, working along a continuum of support. Studies that examine the interactions between tutor and student provide evidence for this notion: they show that effective tutors respond to what the student is attempting to do rather than operating from a preconceived plan for teaching (Hobsbaum, Peters, & Sylva, 1996; Wong et al., 1994). Essentially, effective tutors provide more help when the learner is not successful and less help when the student is successful (Wood, 2003; Wood & Wood, 1996).

LITERACY COACHES SCAFFOLDING TEACHERS

It seems, then, that scaffolding is more than a matter of simply intervening; the quality of the interaction makes a difference to learning, more so than the frequency of the interaction. In other words, a critical feature of assisted learning is not how often help is given, but the kind of help that is given and when it is offered. This finding has important implications for coaching, which we will discuss next; we will also provide some examples from our coaching research.

Varying the Level of Help

In coaching a group of teachers in a professional development session, Mary Fried draws on the principle of varying the level of help in response to the learner. In the example that follows, the teachers are observing another teacher work with a first-grade student who has been experiencing great difficulty learning to read and has fallen far behind his peers. The lesson is going on behind a one-way mirror, so the observers on the other side are free to talk with one another about what they are seeing without interfering with the lesson. This professional development format of observing and discussing a live lesson on the other side of a one-way mirror is a fairly common format in teacher education. The teacher on the other side of the mirror is aware that his or her lesson is being observed; in fact the teacher has brought the student to the professional development session specifically for such observation. We will discuss the use of one-way mirrors a little more in the following chapter.

Mary guides the teachers' observations and coaches their analyses of the teaching and learning going on behind the mirror. To illustrate how coaches can vary their support to teachers, we categorize the kind of help she provides using E. Rodgers's (2004) four levels of support: questioning, directing, demonstrating, and telling.

Example 1. During this first transcript, the student is rereading a familiar story, which is at an easy text level for him.

> MARY: He didn't look and it's very slow. (Telling) How does it sound? (Questioning)
>
> TEACHERS: It's word by word. . . . It's slow. . . . He's not putting it together.
>
> MARY: Yes it is. (Telling) Is this book on the student's cutting edge? Would you agree with the teacher's analysis that his biggest problem is being slow? (Questioning)
>
> TEACHER 1: Yes.
>
> TEACHER 2: It's very slow.
>
> TEACHER 3: The biggest question is, Why?

Mary focuses everyone's attention at the outset by telling them that the student did not look at the print while reading the first page, and she notes that he is reading very slowly. Although she provides the greatest amount of help possible by telling her listeners that the student is reading slowly and neglecting to look at the print, she accomplishes an important goal of focusing everyone's observation on the same feature of the lesson. With their shared attention established, they can collaborate in their analysis of the teaching and learning.

Once the teachers agree that the student is reading too slowly, Mary withdraws her support somewhat by questioning. She does this by asking them whether they agree with the teacher's analysis, provided before the lesson started, that the student's biggest problem is being slow. Everyone agrees, and one teacher raises the provocative question, Why?

Example 2. Notice in the transcript that follows how Mary, as coach, refrains from taking part in the collaborative inquiry by letting the three teachers work together to independently analyze the pace of the student's reading. Teacher 3 continues to press her colleagues to think about why.

During this segment, the student is rereading a second familiar book at an easy level.

> TEACHER 6: He's fast to turn the pages, but slow reading.
>
> TEACHER 3: Why?

TEACHER 5: This is a patterned book and . . .

TEACHER 3: Do you think he should be reading it more phrased then?

TEACHER 5: Yeah, but even the pattern isn't helping him.

MARY: So what is his theory of reading? (Questioning)

TEACHERS: Getting it right.

MARY: Danita [Teacher 3] posed a good question (Directing): Why is he reading slowly, not phrased? Is he not incorporating oral language in his reading? (Questioning)

TEACHER 4: He doesn't have a system.

TEACHER 3: Books at easier levels would let him use his oral language more.

When Mary does come in with support by asking, "So what is his theory of reading?" she does so by questioning the teachers about what they are learning about the student. Her question supports the teachers to pull together their observations of the student and come to a conclusion based on their independent analysis of what they are seeing the student try. By clinching their analysis like this, Mary ensures that the group has a shared understanding about the student as a reader. She then guides the teachers to continue their line of inquiry about why the student might be reading so slowly by returning to the question, "Why is he reading slowly, not phrased?"

We can see that Mary withholds help while the three teachers independently analyze the student's reading and hypothesize about why he isn't reading in a phrased way. She intervenes to pull together their observations ("What's his theory of reading?") and to shift the direction of their analysis ("Danita posed a good question . . ."). The timing of Mary's help serves to encourage the teachers' independent analysis and also to steer their observations along a particular line of inquiry.

It's important to notice not only the kind of support Mary provides, but also when she decides to help. Recall that in Wood and Middleton's (1975) study the kind of help provided mattered more than the frequency of help. In fact, one of the most difficult features of scaffolding might be deciding when to withhold help (Wood, 2003). This means that coaches need to decide not only what to focus on and what kind of support to give (questioning, directing, demonstrating, and telling), but also when and when not to provide help.

Example 3. Now that we have described two features of scaffolding—the kind of help and the timing of help—let's return to the coaching example with Mary. The teachers' observation of the lesson continues with the student's reading a less familiar book that was introduced the previous day and with the teacher taking a running record (see Clay, 2000, for a description of running records). This third book is not as familiar to the student as the previous two and is probably closer to his instructional reading level. By now, approximately 5 minutes have elapsed since the lesson started and the teachers began their observation and discussion.

Notice that Mary provides more help to the teachers in their analysis by shifting from questioning to telling. Think about why she decides to offer more support when she does.

> MARY: His eyes are off the page; I wonder why? (Telling and Questioning)
> TEACHER 7: But he's not appealing for help when his eyes are off the book. He doesn't appeal.
> MARY: It's still problematic because his eyes are not moving forward on the page. (Telling)
> TEACHER 7: He just skipped a whole line.
> MARY: Is that the first directional problem that we have seen? Is that a lapse in direction? (Questioning) [No response]
> MARY: What items on Concepts About Print relate to directional movement? (Questioning)
> TEACHERS: Return sweep . . . left page before right page . . . words out of order . . . letters out of order.
> MARY: So he has a pattern of deliberate pausing; when? (Questioning)
> TEACHER 3: When he looks up.
> MARY: When else? (Questioning)
> TEACHER 3: Return sweep.
> MARY: Beginning of a line, and what about turning a page? (Questioning)
> TEACHER 5: His eyes are on the picture first.
> MARY: That's good processing to glance at the picture first (Telling), but it was on return sweep that he would look also, even when not difficult. (Telling) That's not efficient processing, is it? (Telling) So we know he has some problems with directionality and that return sweep is not automatic for him. (Telling)

Analyzing How the Coach Varied the Level of Help. In this set of interactions, Mary supports the teachers' thinking and analyses to come to the understanding that the student has not yet brought directionality under control. He does not automatically use return sweep to go to the first word on the next line, and it appears to be an effort for him to follow the print in a left-right, top-bottom direction. As many teachers know, it is not unusual for students just emerging into conventional literacy to find directionality challenging. The young reader has to develop concepts about how print operates, regardless of the language (see Clay, 2001, for more information). Let's see how Mary scaffolds the teachers' thinking to arrive at this hypothesis.

She begins by telling the teachers that the student's eyes are off the text. There's probably little to be gained by questioning them about where the student's eyes are; not only is this an odd-sounding question, it might slow up the analysis. It's important to notice that the student is not looking at the print, and Mary tells them so. The teachers now have some common ground, a focus, to continue their collaborative inquiry.

Mary shifts to less support when she asks, "I wonder why?" This open-ended question is at a very high level. The teachers are invited to share in the wondering, to inquire, and to offer their analysis. The first response to this wondering question is that as long as the student is not appealing for help, it doesn't really matter that he's not looking at the print. This response signals to Mary that she must provide more support. The teacher does not see the significance of Mary's observation and is ready to dismiss the student's tendency to look away from the print as unimportant. Mary responds with more support by telling, saying that it is problematic because the student is not processing the text if he's not looking at the print.

It's around this time in the transcript that we can tell that Mary is really working on the teachers' cutting edge. When one teacher observes that the student skipped a whole line, Mary responds with the question, "Is that the first directional problem that we have seen?" For the first time there is no response to a question, suggesting that the teachers aren't sure. Perhaps they don't know what directional problems look like, and they need some more time to process this question. Mary, through her questioning and telling, has brought the teachers to the edge of their knowing. Their silence suggests that they need support to keep this analysis moving forward; they can't do it without Mary.

It's interesting that at this point Mary doesn't resort to telling. She could have simply told them examples of directional problems, but presumably this would have provided more support than she wanted to provide. Instead, she continues to question them about directionality, linking to something they already know about: the "Concepts About Print" task (from Clay's *An Observation Survey of Early Literacy Achievement* [2002]). By doing this, Mary steps back into their realm of knowledge and helps them link what they already know about directionality to their observations of this student, who has by now read three books. We can surmise that Mary's coaching has lifted the teachers' understanding about directionality.

Mary will no doubt go on to link the teachers' observations that the student was reading slowly together with their shared analysis that the student has not yet brought return sweep and other directionality behaviors under control.

Learning from 10 Minutes of Coaching. These interactions between Mary and a group of teachers observing a tutoring session lasted just 10 minutes, yet they provide a good example of scaffolding. We see that Mary is helping the teachers complete a task that they couldn't do at the same level without assistance; in fact we can tell when she reaches the edges of their knowing—their zone of proximal development.

Mary guides them to observe closely and collect evidence from the lesson. The evidence that they collect (skipping a line, looking up from the text at the end of a line instead of automatically going to the left and down to the next word) allows the teachers to conclude that the student does have problems with directionality. The teachers' comments are grounded in this shared example.

Mary also varies her support by shifting from questioning to telling. We can see that even her questions vary in their level of support ("I wonder why . . ." and "What items relate to directionality?"). Even though she relied on just two kinds of support, telling and questioning, during this 10-minute coaching snippet, the kind of support that she offers varies in response to what the teachers know and are trying to understand. Most important, Mary is not following a preconceived plan, script, or set of responses; instead she is supporting the teachers in the moment.

If she thought more help was needed, Mary could have demonstrated for the teachers by working with the student on the other side of the mirror while the teachers observed. In fact, in a section that follows, we discuss the peril and promise of demonstrating. No doubt the teachers would have seen some explicit teaching on learning how to look at print, such as going to the next word then to the left and down without looking away from the print when the student reached the end of a line. This might have given the teachers an opportunity to test out their theory that the student was still working on directionality while reading and that it was not yet automatic.

As we can see from Mary's coaching, it is possible to follow the essential rule of scaffolding—provide less help when the learner is experiencing success, more when the learner runs into difficulty—within a coaching setting. The coach can demonstrate for the teacher, then shift to questioning, and come back to demonstrating—all within the space of a few minutes. In fact, the coach makes all these decisions about the kind of help to offer in the moment in response to how the teacher is participating in the activity. By interacting in this responsive way, the coach is able to work in the teacher's zone of proximal development even while the teacher maintains an active role in the process.

Demonstrating: The Peril and Promise

Teachers speak enthusiastically about the value of demonstration, identifying it as a powerful form of support to help them take on something new or redirect their own practice (E. Rodgers, Fullerton, & DeFord, 2001). There are two important issues for a literacy coach to consider here, though: one that relates to the teacher, and the other to the coach.

While demonstrating is a legitimate and important kind of help to scaffold learning, it should be used with caution. This form of help by definition positions the learner as a passive observer and the coach as taking on the teacher's role. We know from Wood and Middleton's (1975) research that relying on this much help can have a disastrous effect. The learner (in this context, the teacher) may decide that the shift in teaching is too great to take on and become convinced that the gap between the teacher's current practice and what the coach is demonstrating is too wide to bridge. If you've ever watched someone whom you perceive to be an expert demonstrate something for you and thought, "I'll never be able to do that," then you can relate to this rationale. There seems to be an inherent value in trying something yourself and having an opportunity to learn from your attempts, particularly the half rights or nearly theres!

There is support for this notion that it's important to be actively involved in order to facilitate learning. Bruner describes how infants learn a skilled action, such as grasping an object, by describing it as a set of attempts that are refined by feedback with each try, until eventually the child has internalized the act of reaching and grasping (Bruner in Clay, 1991). If the child were to observe an adult reaching and grasping a glass, there would be feedback to receive and the child could modify subsequent attempts, which are critical features of learning a skilled action. While some might argue that teaching is not quite the same as learning a skilled action, there is still, we think, a case to be made for being actively involved in order for the learner to change participation in the activity.

So even though demonstrating might be just the kind of support that some teachers prefer, our understanding of learning theory suggests to us that coaches should not overly rely on it. Rather, it seems more important to vary the kind of help offered in response to the learner's participation in the activity.

The other issue related to demonstrating has to do with the coach. We have found in our experience that coaches are actually more likely not to demonstrate something for the teacher than they are to demonstrate, despite the high value that many teachers appear to put on demonstrations. For most people, ourselves included, it seems to require enormous energy and courage to take the teacher's role and do the teaching. In our work coaching coaches, we find we often need to provide extra support and encouragement to coaches in order to help them feel confident enough to demonstrate for the teacher. In the example that follows, a teacher leader (a Reading Recovery coach) reflects on a demonstration that she provided for teachers during a professional development session.

> During the [professional development session] it became apparent that the child needed to move up book levels. During the new-book portion of the lesson, I worked with the student and moved the child from a Level 3 to a Level 6 [while the teachers observed on the other side of a one-way mirror]. This greatly influenced the discussion as we [the group of teachers and the coach] talked about why I had done this and had a wonderful discussion about acceleration and the urgency to teach our children. . . . After doing this I really felt like the group made a big shift in their thinking, and while I didn't think it was my best book introduction, it did accomplish my goal: to get the teachers to reflect on children's acceleration and how we need to stay on the cutting edge of their learning. While I am still not comfortable with demonstrating during a teacher's lesson, I do see that I need to continue to do this and not let an opportunity pass. . . . The teachers and students cannot wait! (Donna, Reading Recovery teacher leader)

Perhaps the most important point to note here is not that the coach worked with the student in order to provide a perfect model of teaching—that wasn't the goal. Rather, it is important to note that she provided the teachers with another shared example (along with the lesson they had observed) to discuss. We think this is the real value of a demonstration. Teachers can be provided with an alternative case, and these alternatives can fuel discussion and analysis in the same way that the coach described.

Providing Opportunities for Participation

A common theme across the previous two sections is the emphasis on participation, yet our description of how the teachers observed a live lesson while the coach guided their observations and analyses is not a typical professional development scenario. In fact, according to a recent national survey of reading directors:

> Across the country, one-shot professional development experiences continue to be the most common form of delivering information to teachers. About half the school districts indicated they did provide some multi-day workshops and follow-up, although this usually took the form of "Call if you have questions." Within traditional sit-and-get workshops, the contact time between the presenter and the teacher is minimal, and the teachers are generally only given handouts and contact information to help them put it all together in their classrooms. (Hughes, Cash, Ahwee, & Klingner, 2002, p. 24)

If Mary had worked with the teachers in a more typical, one-shot professional development setting, she likely would have started out with a presentation on directionality and then showed a video of a student reading aloud. She probably would have asked the teachers to jot down, while they viewed the videotape, examples of the student having difficulty with directionality. Following the videotape, Mary would then have asked the teachers for their observations and linked their comments back to her presentation.

While this mode of working with teachers might be easier for the staff developer, we just can't imagine such a scenario ever resulting in the richness of analysis that we saw in the 10 minutes of coaching that Mary provided. Under those all-too-common scenarios of typical professional development, teachers rarely have an opportunity to participate; yet as we described earlier, participation is key to learning—not only for the learner but also for the coach who is pitching the help.

Coaches can also provide an opportunity for teachers to be actively involved in a different format: that of working one-to-one during a school visit. This format involves the coach going out to the school to observe the teacher working with a group of students. In this case, only the coach works with the teacher. A variation of this has the coach going to the school with a small group of teachers, perhaps two or three only, to observe a lesson. Usually there is a specific purpose in mind for these group visits. In Chapter 5 we described possible formats for school visits and discussed issues involved with this type of coaching format.

In any case, whether the coach is working one-to-one with a teacher or working with a small group, the emphasis here is on active participation. Of course there is still the risk that even in the kinds of coaching settings we describe, teachers can still take a passive role. In Chapter 7 we describe how the coach might guide inquiry so that all teachers are involved in the discussion.

Clay (1988) writes about learning through action in her chapter "From Acts to Awareness," describing how children emerge into literacy through their involvement with print. The same rationale can be applied to other learning situations. Teachers who are learning how to teach in Reading Recovery, for example, start teaching children right away while they are still learning the teaching procedures and theories behind the instruction. They do not spend a month studying how to teach before teaching; they start working with students on the first day. There is great value in participating in the activity to be learned in order to learn more deeply about it.

CONCLUSION

We began this chapter with a definition of learning and with a description of some of the essential features of scaffolding. We suggest ways in which literacy coaches can think about the kind of help they provide to teachers, the amount of support they provide, and when to offer help in order to scaffold teacher learning and reach greater depths of understanding. The principles we describe apply whether the coach is working one to one with a teacher or working with a small group of teachers.

The value of a shared experience cannot be understated, whether it is provided by a video, or a live lesson that is taught while a coach or group of teachers observe. The shared experience provides real, concrete examples for discussion, and teachers can ground their analysis in what they have seen. It's hard to speak only in the abstract when others can press for evidence or provide counterexamples that everyone has observed.

There is, however, greater potential to shift understanding when a group is involved in the observation, as opposed to a coach's working with just one teacher on a school visit. With a group, there are more participants to contribute to the collaborative inquiry; with a coach and just one teacher, there are only two people to share in the analysis. In addition, a live example is probably better than viewing a videotape because teachers are more likely to be actively engaged. Videotapes create a more passive setting for learning, we think, than a live lesson.

We do not provide a menu of responses. Coaches who effectively scaffold understandings are ready to respond to the learner; this means making decisions about the kind of help to offer and when to offer it—in the moment—for coaches in order to pitch their help at just the right level of sensitivity. In what follows, we provide a list of the features of scaffolding involved in coaching analyses of teaching.

- Provide opportunities for meaningful participation.
- Observe changes in teacher participation in analysis.
- Calibrate the kind of help offered.
- Work along a continuum of support.
- Consider the timing of the help.
- Bring teachers to the edge of their knowing.
- Focus observations, guide interactions, and tie up analysis.

There can be no preconceived plan for these kinds of meaningful interactions. The only requirement is a thoughtful coach who creates settings that require active participation and then observes the participation closely in order to provide the kind of help that is on the teacher's cutting edge of learning.

CHAPTER 7

Guiding Group Discussions

Teachers working together in small groups, observing each other teach, holding their practice up for close observation, analyzing their teaching and the teaching of others—most would agree that this kind of work is anathema to the usual forms of teacher professional development. After intense preservice teacher experiences featuring microteaching, videotaping, self-analysis, journaling, supervision, and feedback, inservice teachers rarely have other opportunities in their professional lives to observe themselves teach—or to see anyone else teach, for that matter. Indeed, Wilson and Daviss (1994) questioned whether and how education can ever change when teachers rarely have an opportunity to talk to one another and work together around their professional practices. On the other hand, the authors argue that it is precisely that spirit of inquiry and testing new approaches that leads to innovations and improved designs in everything from toothbrushes and kettles to bridges and airplanes. As long as teachers work in relative isolation, redesign in education is unlikely.

New teachers typically show up on the first day of school wondering what to teach; how to maintain classroom control while encouraging participation; how to assess; and most of all, how to teach like the experienced teachers on staff. Adrian, one of the authors of this volume, recalls just this kind of experience in his first few months as a new high school English teacher. His first teaching evaluation included comments that the clock was not flush to the wall and that several hooks on the classroom drapes were out of place, making the curtains droop. There was little feedback on his teaching and no opportunity for him to work with and learn from others to develop his craft. So Adrian took matters into his own hands and arranged to spend his preparation time in the classrooms of experienced teachers—teachers whom he had identified as having it all together. He also arranged to talk with other English teachers about how they planned instruction and managed classroom organization.

Many educators can relate to Adrian's experience. It is unusual for teachers to work together in groups on their practice, yet when they do, remarkable innovations happen. Literacy Collaborative, a framework for literacy classroom instruction that is implemented in classrooms across the United States, began with a few teachers regularly getting together in small groups to discuss their teaching practices. The framework for Reading Recovery lessons (an early literacy intervention for first-grade students) is grounded in basic research (see Clay, 2001), but it was developed and refined as a result of discussion among teachers as they observed other teachers' trial procedures behind a one-way mirror.

In this chapter we work from our case study research and our review of related literature to describe principles of coaching small groups of teachers, who form communities of learners and inquirers around their practice. We draw from Lyons's (1993, 1994) work to describe how group inquiry can be scaffolded by a coach. We also describe exemplary practices of coaches who support teachers in going beyond surface-level comments to sharing inquiry that brings the group to new understandings about teaching and learning. These small groups of teachers talking to other teachers, led by a knowledgeable and supportive coach, exemplify the spirit of inquiry that Wilson and Daviss (1994) propose can lead to redesign in education.

A FRAMEWORK FOR SCAFFOLDING GROUP INQUIRY

Lyons (1994) noted the value of coaching teachers in small groups:

> Teachers consult with each other to develop a theoretical base that is grounded in action. [In a coaching setting] they are encourage[d] to approximate, to generate a hypothesis about what the student has learned and controls, to challenge one another, and to provide alternative explanations for the student's behavior with supporting evidence for their hypothesis. (p. 285)

Maloch's (2002) research on classroom discussion groups suggested, however, that it is challenging for small groups of learners to scaffold their discussion. The students in Maloch's study needed to first learn how to learn from each other and how to interact in order to scaffold one another to new insights and understandings. Although the teacher's input and level of support decreased over time as the students became increasingly more able to carry on their discussion, they continued to need some level of teacher involvement to nudge their inquiry forward.

We think the same might be true about small groups of teachers working together. A coach's role in guiding group discussion is integral, especially early on as the teachers take on new teaching strategies, but the coach is not the central figure in the inquiry process. We agree with

Lambert et al. (1995), who apply theories of constructivist learning to leading and note:

> In order to lead conversations that can lead to professional cultures, educators need to construct understandings about the nature of constructivist conversations and acquire facilitation skills in order to convene, move, and deepen our talk together. (p. 101)

In other words, the coach needs to share with the group members how they are expected to interact to support each other's learning, and the coach needs to become skillful at facilitating discussion so that the entire group can work together toward deeper understandings in this unique setting. As we discussed in Chapter 6, once teachers have the *how* and *what* of teaching under way, the coach's role should shift to one of facilitator of inquiry.

Scaffolding group discussion in this way is not an easy task. The challenges are different from working one to one with teachers on school visits, but the possibilities for change are greatly expanded with the addition of more people to the inquiry. We next describe several features of coaching small teacher-inquiry groups that we think will be useful for coaches in thinking about their work.

Grounding Inquiry in Observation of Student Learning

Lyons (1993) explained that one of the first things teachers new to a coaching situation need to do is

> divorce themselves from an instructional stance that champions a sequence of skills, and instead, respond to what they see a child doing while reading and writing. That is, teachers need to abandon preconceived ideas about the nature of beginning reading instruction, from a published program for example, and learn to observe what the child is doing in his or her attempts to become literate. (p. 325)

The best way into reflecting on and recomprehending teaching, then, is through shared examples of children being taught rather than stand-and-deliver kinds of presentations.

Placing children's learning at the center of this professional development work means that the coach will have to arrange for small groups of teachers to observe teaching. There are several formats that can be used to make this happen. Teachers may get together with a coach at one school to observe a lesson being taught, or if the district has a room with a one-way mirror installed, the lesson can be viewed there.

For some teachers who may not have used one-way mirrors before, this might conjure up images of television crime dramas. When one-way mirrors are used in the school setting, nothing could be further from the truth. One-way mirrors are often used in educational settings, and their purpose is to allow groups of teachers and their coach to observe live teaching of students and discuss what they see while it occurs. Since this group both prebriefs and debriefs with the teacher who teaches the lesson, the teacher is not only aware of the comments but also responds to the discussion after the lesson has been taught. Since over the course of a year all teachers might be observed using the one-way mirror technique, the emphasis of the discussion is on the development of high-quality observations and understandings regarding teaching.

A substitute for a live experience may consist of viewing a videotape of a lesson and then discussing it together afterward. There are, however, a few disadvantages to using a videotape instead of a live lesson. One is that the teachers' observations of interactions are limited to where the camera was looking at any particular time while the lesson was being taped. There may be important interactions, comments, or events in the classroom that go unrecorded by the camera that the teachers would have picked up on had they been free to observe the experience live. Also, we hypothesize that observing a videotape of a lesson places the viewer in a passive mode, much as in watching a television show or a movie. A live lesson, we think, is a much more engaging experience for the observer. If the live lesson can be observed behind a one-way mirror, the observers can even talk during the lesson.

Whether the small group of teachers observe a lesson on videotape, live in a classroom, or behind a one-way mirror, they will have an opportunity to develop theories about teaching and learning that are grounded in real examples of teaching. The important point is that the coach guide their observations, as Lyons says (1994), to

- Generate a hypothesis about what the student has learned and controls
- Challenge one another's hypotheses
- Provide alternative explanations for the student's behavior

While this takes place, the coach should offer evidence from the lesson to support their analysis. Undertaking this critical work, Lyons (1993) explained, will help teachers

become more skillful in (a) observing and analyzing a student's behaviors, (b) deciding what the student needed to learn how to do, and (c) determining the appropriate question to support the student's growing competencies. (p. 326)

Supporting Inquiry Through Varied Discussion Formats

One of the difficulties in using group discussion is that there is a tendency to just sit and talk. This is problematic because the activity quickly becomes routinized, does not especially promote inquiry, and is vulnerable to domination by a vocal minority or an individual. It is essential, therefore, that coaches vary the discussion format of the small group work.

Buzz Groups. In a *buzz group* participants sit in small groups of two or three to discuss an issue or question for 5 or 10 minutes. The power of the buzz group lies in the security of trying out an idea with a neighbor before presenting it in front of the whole group. Additionally, because language mediates thinking (Vygotsky, 1978), when several individuals have an opportunity to talk with each other ideas can be clarified, expanded, and enriched. Using buzz groups helps to individualize the use of the group in a way that cannot be accomplished when the whole group talks together.

Pairs Discuss. In the *pairs discuss* approach, participants are paired together and discuss their ideas with one another. After 5 or 10 minutes each pair is partnered with another pair, and the group of four discuss. The power of the pairs discuss model lies in the graduated support it provides to each individual in sharing ideas as they move from a smaller group to a larger one. The other benefit is that as the group grows larger, new questions emerge that can be brought back to the whole group for later discussion.

Two Groups. In the *two groups* approach the participants are typically divided into groups. One group works on one question or issue, and the other group works on another question or issue. After the initial discussion the two groups share. The strength of the two groups approach lies in the ability to tap the power of a group of individuals without having the issues associated with small group work. The two groups approach is also a great time-saver, since twice as much work can be accomplished.

Scaffolding of Inquiry by the Coach

A tenet of the small-group discussion is that language mediates thought. To that end, everyone in a small group should contribute at some level to the discussion. This responsibility to talk helps to ensure that each participant has an opportunity to reformulate or think through an idea, either by using one's own language to mediate an idea or through using someone else's language. This concept is familiar to most people—after all, who hasn't experienced the spark of a new idea based on something that someone else has said? Talk is central to thinking and learning.

A role of the coach is make this responsibility clear to the group participants and then work to support participation from all. Typically we have not had a problem with one participant responding too much, but we often note that some individuals do not respond very much or at all. Perhaps they are quiet Einsteins with good ideas to share if given an opening to do so. To help solicit these comments some coaches we know talk beforehand with more vocal participants and suggest that they hold their comments or questions until others contribute, thereby creating an opportunity for those who are less vocal.

Heather, a novice coach who was introduced in Chapter 2, reflected on her efforts in this regard following a coaching visit from Emily. Heather wrote:

> Emily debriefed with me about getting everyone in the group
> to become more active participants in the discussions . . . and at
> the circle. She made me more aware that sometimes these people
> are the most thoughtful, analytical members of the group, and
> if they share their thoughts and observations, they may lift the
> understanding of the whole group. These rationales make so
> much sense. Nichelle, Desiree, and Hali are my low responders.
> They are also my best teachers. They shift after every school visit.
> They are analytical in their discussions with me one to one—why
> wouldn't they contribute at the same high level in small groups?
> I can't assume too much, so I have shifted in my process and
> have spoken to each of them individually. So far, there has been
> a small shift, but my expectations are high and I will continue to
> push for change.

Later, as Heather continued to reflect on the important role of talk in supporting group inquiry, she wrote:

> After listening to 2 weeks' worth of audiotaped small-group
> sessions, I realized that the teachers are taking too many notes
> and not reflecting and listening to each other. I'm going to begin
> tomorrow's group with these expectations: no notes, observe,
> listen to each other, initiate questions, and participate in the
> problem solving. I am also guilty of getting sidetracked and will

leave the notes behind to be a better observer and listener and really follow the group.

The coach has a pivotal role in supporting everyone in contributing to the group inquiry process and in making this process visible to all participants so that they are aware of their role. Getting this process going may take an explicit conversation with the group members, as Heather planned to do the following day, but the way the coach and teachers interact together in small groups should change over time.

Changing Inquiry Over Time

As we discussed in Chapter 2, our understanding of learning is informed by a Vygotskian (1978) view of development; that is, learning can be defined by changing participation in an activity. From this perspective, then, if there is learning going on, we would expect change over time in both how the coach coaches and how the teachers participate in the analysis of teaching.

These kinds of shifts have been documented in Lyons's (1993) research. The teachers in her study moved from initially simply describing student behavior, to inferring the students' perceptual and cognitive processing from their observations, and then to identifying appropriate teaching procedures to scaffold student learning. The way they interacted also shifted from providing one response to a coach's question to constructing what Lyons (1994) called "chains of reasoning." In these chains, teachers made as many as six or seven contributions to the inquiry before the coach came into the discussion with a comment or question to nudge the inquiry along.

The coach's participation shifted as well. Early on the coach worked to support the teachers' inquiry by expanding, clarifying, restating, and weaving together teachers' comments. After about 6 months of coaching, the coach worked in a different way, contributing less and with fewer turns in the discussion. The coach, Lyons (1994) hypothesized, relinquished leadership in the inquiry, while the teachers took on a greater role in guiding the discussion. The teachers had learned how to structure their own learning but like the teachers in Maloch's (2002) study, we hypothesize that they will continue to need the coach's help to support and guide their inquiry.

Although we do not have supporting evidence yet, we surmise that the teachers' participation in the inquiry might not have changed if the coach did not relinquish leadership and change. In other words, had the coach continued to guide the group's inquiry with the same level of involvement and turn taking, the teachers might not have taken on a greater role in the discussion. We coach coaches to deliberately think about how they will change their role and prepare teachers to take on a different role in the discussion. Bonnie, a coach we met in Chapter 2, reflected on her efforts to do just that; her thoughts echo the challenge of turning the discussion over to the teachers.

> I was telling instead of providing opportunities for teachers to discuss. I was unaware of my control until I heard myself on tape. I have managed to make progress in this area, by becoming aware of when I'm about to respond and making myself pause a couple of beats to think of the best approach to get the teachers involved. My role needs to shift to engaging the group in commenting on their observations and citing their evidence. This approach frees me up to listen, comment, and share rather than working hard at thinking about what question to ask next. (Bonnie, literacy coach)

Bonnie is developing her ability to reflect-in-action (see the discussion in Chapter 5). She is analyzing her leading in the moment while she is guiding the discussion to change her coaching style. It is challenging, however, to know when to listen and when to comment. This is perhaps not surprising given what we know about the nature of scaffolding decision making. As Wood (2003) noted, scaffolding involves decisions about what to teach, how to teach, and when to teach; Wood emphasized that the *when* decision is probably the toughest of the three.

Example 1. In the case example that we provide next, a small group of teachers, B.B., Koko, Millie, and Lou, are observing a live lesson being taught behind a one-way mirror. The student is rereading familiar books; the teacher's goal is to teach the student to read in a phrased and fluent way. While the teachers watch the lesson, their observations and conversation are guided by a novice coach. As you read, think about when you might expect the coach to come into the conversation with a nudge to help guide the teachers' thinking about the student's fluency. Notice Millie's concern, which goes unaddressed in the conversation.

COACH: How does the reading sound?
B.B.: I think it sounds phrased.
KOKO: Did you? I thought it sounded a little robotic. Maybe there was some patchy phrasing here or there. [The student continues to read.] That's a bit better. That sounded more phrased.

MILLIE: I wonder how long he has been reading books at that
level?

B.B.: He's getting on a roll now. It's sounding more phrased.

LOU: That's what reading familiar books is for—to learn how to
read in a fluent way.

KOKO: But that part sounded robotic again, didn't it?

MILLIE: Is it too high a level for familiar books for him?

COACH: What do you think of the teacher's choice of books for
familiar reading?

The teachers are actively contributing to the inquiry but the discussion
does not seem to be moving forward as it would in Lyons's (1994) chains
of reasoning metaphor. Even though the teachers have put forward several different ideas, the discussion does not seem to be very productive; the
teachers seem to be in need of a coach to do something with their theories.
They have contributed eight times since the coach's initial question about
how the reading sounded, but they seem to be meandering in their thinking, judging the student's fluency differently almost with each phrase that
the student reads.

We do not mean that the teachers all have to agree with one another all
the time. In fact, the best discussions occur when diverging views are ex-
pressed. Within these moments the coach can nudge the group to provide
evidence, to think about why the student might be able to read one page
more fluently than the next, or to consider Millie's question and discuss
the features of text that support fluent reading. The goal is not necessarily
to agree, but to keep going with the inquiry (Lindfors, 1999).

Example 2. As we outlined in Chapter 5, the coach can nudge the inquiry in several different ways: through questioning assumptions, helping
the teachers to identify alternatives, supporting the teachers in weighing
options, deliberating with the teachers on how to proceed, and making
decisions on courses of action for teaching.

We replay the interactions between the coach and teachers B.B., Lou,
and Koko, and this time we offer suggestions for what the coach might
have said and when the coach might have intervened in order to support
the teachers in going further and deeper with their analysis. The suggestions are written in italics, and we provide several possible contributions
for the coach.

COACH: How does the reading sound?

B.B.: I think it sounds phrased.

KOKO: Did you? I thought it sounded a little robotic. Maybe there
was some patchy phrasing here or there.

[At this point, the coach might have intervened to scaffold their inquiry.]

COACH: *What might the teacher do at this point when the fluency became problematic for the student? Let's think of two or three different things that the teacher can try to support the student.*

[Or the coach might have said:]

COACH: *Where did you think the student was more phrased, Koko?*

[Or the coach might have said:]

COACH: *Let's listen to the student read two more pages and then I'll ask each person to rate his fluency on a scale of 1 to 10. Be prepared to give some evidence for your rating.*

In our alternative scenarios, the coach comes in a little sooner and takes advantage of the diverging points of view to support the teachers in going further with their analyses. At some point in the discussion, the teachers may have to come to a consensus overall about whether the teacher needs to continue to support the student's fluency, and they might even go on to outline the elements of a plan for the student's lesson the next day.

Another possible time for the coach to come into the discussion to nudge the inquiry might have been after Millie posed her first question about text level. Even though she poses her question as "I wonder"—a very nice invitation to others to explore a different line of inquiry—the teachers do not respond. At the same time diverging views are appearing about the student's fluency.

Example 3. We offer several other possibilities and a new entry point for the coach as we continue the replay of the interaction.

KOKO: That's a bit better. That sounded more phrased.

MILLIE: I wonder how long he has been reading books at that level?

[Here the coach might have scaffolded the inquiry by saying:]

COACH: *Millie, tell us why you are wondering about the level of the text?*

[Or the coach might have said:]

COACH: *Let's talk about why text level matters.*

[Or the coach might have said:]

COACH: *It's not so much the level that matters, Millie. What is it about the text itself that can have an impact on a student's fluency?*

[Or simply:]

COACH: *Say more about that, Millie.*

We should mention at this point that our suggestions obviously come with the benefit of hindsight; it is much easier to consider alternative coaching moves after the session rather than in the moment. The coach in our example is new to the role and is learning how to guide the inquiry of a small group of teachers, a daunting task under any circumstance. It takes some practice, continued analysis (preferably of audiotapes of one's guiding a discussion), and reflection for a coach to be able to expertly and quickly reflect-in-action to make decisions about how to scaffold, what to scaffold, and especially *when* to scaffold small-group discussion.

Our example in Chapter 6 of Mary Fried guiding a small-group discussion shows how expert coaches can become at guiding small group discussion. Notice in that discussion when Mary comes into the inquiry and how she supports their hypothesis making. She guides them to new insights through her well-placed comments and questions.

> TEACHER 6: He's fast to turn the pages, but slow reading.
> TEACHER 3: Why?
> TEACHER 5: This is a patterned book and . . .
> TEACHER 3: Do you think he should be reading it more phrased then?
> TEACHER 5: Yeah, but even the pattern isn't helping him.
> MARY: So what is his theory of reading? (Questioning)

Mary enters the conversation at a pivotal moment. The teachers are sharing their observations about the student; Mary's question about his theory of reading requires them to weigh what they have been observing and come to some conclusion together, based on their evidence. Without her question to tie up their observations, they might simply continue to share comments about the reading. Later she works in an optimal way to pose the right question at the right time:

> MARY: Danita [Teacher 3] posed a good question (Directing): Why is he reading slowly, not phrased? Is he not incorporating oral language in his reading? (Questioning)
> TEACHER 4: He doesn't have a system.
> TEACHER 3: Books at easier levels would let him use his oral language more.

Getting just the right probe at just the right time is an incredibly difficult thing to do in a live coaching session, but it is the kind of skill coaches can develop over time, as Mary demonstrates so well in the example.

Lyons's (1994) concept of collectively constructing chains of reasoning is a valuable one here because it helps coaches to understand the work that they need to undertake to help teachers in "observing, analyzing, and discussing student-teacher interactions in progress" (p. 286). The implication for coaches working with small groups of teachers is that the interactions within the group should change over time as the teachers take on a greater role in the discussion; the coach is responsible for creating this shift in participation.

> Leading the conversations is at the heart of constructivist leadership. It is the facilitation of the reciprocal processes that enable participants in an educational community to construct meanings towards a common purpose for teaching and learning. It is a skilled undertaking for which each participant needs to be prepared; it is a shared responsibility. (Lambert et al., 1995, p. 102)

The degree to which the coach addresses and follows up on issues raised in the small group depends on the nature of the issues. Things that can be sorted out quickly are dealt with on the spot. Things that require more time can be examined more carefully during the discussion.

CONCLUSION

In many ways, small-group work is the cornerstone of coaching conversations among teachers. It is difficult to do, since scaffolding conversation as it unfolds is tricky. For this reason, discussion formats can be used as a tool to support deep thinking about teaching. By using these formats over time, constructivist dialogue about teaching can be built.

In Chapter 9 we will suggest that debriefings that occur when a coach visits one teacher should be shorter rather than longer, but in small-group sessions it is possible to have either longer debriefings or numerous shorter debriefings. This is possible because there are many teachers sharing the intense work of reflecting and because the coach can structure the session to support their inquiry work.

CHAPTER 8

Using Questions to Think About Teaching

You can ask anyone a question and obtain a response, but asking questions as part of coaching conversations must be undertaken with great care. The literacy coach needs to solicit conversation by making initial probes regarding teacher knowledge or understandings or by probing emerging decision making by teachers. Additionally, the literacy coach has the option to probe two groups: the teacher who is teaching and the observers watching the teaching. Of course a coach might also probe his or her own understandings through reflection, which we discussed in Chapter 5. The purpose of these probes, then, is to ascertain the teachers' current levels of understanding so that the coach can support the building of additional understanding. Probes act to recruit teachers into conversation about the nature of teaching and learning.

Typically a coach will probe for understandings by devising questions and posing them to the teacher or the observers, but this is problematic. Since questions are a particular kind of probe, they raise two challenges. One is that teachers may respond to the question rather than to the larger enterprise of contributing to dialogue. When teachers respond in this way the coach may, in turn, try to build on the conversation by evaluating the response. In attempting to promote conversation, the coach inadvertently has initiated an initiate-respond-evaluate (IRE) cycle that is likely to repeat itself (Cazden, 1983, 1986). While IRE cycles certainly move conversation forward, they do not promote depth or careful examination. The IRE cycle situates the coach as the source of knowledge and detracts from the co-constructed dialogue that the literacy coach seeks.

A second challenge created by questions is that they may cause teachers to respond in a judgmental way. Below we imagine a coach who poses a seemingly innocuous question and provide some hypothetical teacher responses:

COACH: So, how do you think that lesson went?
TEACHER: I thought it was pretty good. I liked the child's response to my writing prompt.

> OBSERVER: I really liked how you wrote the prompt on the board
>   and gave her time to think about her response.
> TEACHER: If I did it again, I would ask the child to write three
>   sentences.
> COACH: Great! I see you're really trying to build your student's
>   writing.

In this hypothetical case, the IRE components of the conversation are pretty clear. We can also see how the teacher has judged her work and how the observer has augmented this judgment. In fact, when we work with preservice and inservice teachers we find that their analysis of teaching is often similar across both groups. When responding to questions, conversations tend to follow an IRE pattern, are judgmental, feature an observer who will praise the teacher, and feature a teacher who will make a surface-level comment on how he or she would change the teaching next time.

In this chapter we share our thoughts on this very difficult work not as a model, but in the spirit of an initial attempt to build deeper conversations about teaching and learning. We begin by discussing the work of Morgan and Saxton (1994), who contributed significantly to thinking about how to ask better questions. We then share the work of teachers and coaches who have tried to debrief teaching with the goal of using questions to get at deep levels of talking and thinking about teaching.

ASKING BETTER QUESTIONS

A few years back Morgan and Saxton (1994) wrote a very helpful book titled *Asking Better Questions.* Although the book is intended to help teachers think more carefully about the kinds of questions they ask of their school-aged students, as college instructors we have been drawn to the text again and again. Indeed the art of posing questions receives scant attention by instructors of adults, yet instructors rely on this practice heavily (Bean, 2001). Morgan and Saxton draw heavily from the work of Bloom and Krathwohl (1965), providing a detailed way of thinking about questions, generating them, awaiting response, and posing subsequent questions.

Exercising Thinking Skills by Posing Questions

Morgan and Saxton (1994) proposed six kinds of thinking skills that could be exercised by posing different types of questions:

- questions drawing on knowledge (remembering)
- questions which test comprehension (understanding)
- questions which require application (solving)
- questions which encourage analysis (reasoning)
- questions which invite synthesis (creating), and
- questions which promote evaluation (judging). (pp. 12–13)

We see a high degree of overlap when we compare this way of looking at questions and the kinds of work required of teachers and the coach. Certainly coaches may prompt teachers to draw on their knowledge of a student regarding the student's in-class performance or on the teacher's knowledge of how the student performed on an assessment. Coaches, especially with novice teachers, may need to test their comprehension to determine what kind of coaching is required. Coaches obviously call on teachers to apply what has been learned in coaching sessions and, in doing so, learn the degree to which the teachers are able to understand and implement the goals of the coaching initiative. Coaches require teachers to analyze results and observations of teaching, and in so doing they need to scaffold teacher reasoning as a part of the analytical process. As teachers work together in the coaching process, they synthesize results and create theories regarding their teaching and its effects on student learning. Finally, notably at year-end, teachers must evaluate the results of their efforts to change their teaching and their personal teaching goals for the next year. Indeed, just as we have summarized the tasks that are undertaken by teachers, many similar tasks are also undertaken by coaches. Therefore Morgan and Saxton's (1994) framework is extremely helpful for thinking about how we can frame questions to support the teacher and coach as they work together.

Using Categories of Questions to Prompt Teacher Thinking

In addition to discussing six kinds of questions, Morgan and Saxton (1994) also proposed questions that could serve different functions. Some functions are more useful for coaches than others, so we provide the most helpful categories in Figure 8.1. Let's look at these categories in more detail and explain how they're useful for coaches.

Questions Eliciting Information. We can imagine that in a coaching session, coaches and teachers might pose many questions based on eliciting information. For example, questions that focus on facts might include

- What did the student score on the Oral Reading Inventory?
- When was the student selected for reading intervention?
- What do the state guidelines provide for this student?

Figure 8.1: Functions of Questions to Prompt Teacher Thinking

Category of Question	Selected functions of the question
Questions eliciting information	• Focusing on facts • Suggesting implications • Revealing experience
Questions shaping understanding	• Focusing on connections • Pressing for rethinking or restating • Promoting point of view • Demanding interpretation
Questions pressing for reflection	• Developing hypotheses • Focusing on future action • Developing critical assessment

Source: Morgan & Saxton, 1994

Questions that suggest implications might include,

- How have similar students fared without one-to-one coaching?
- Are you prepared to provide this student with a one-to-one reading intervention after school?

Finally, questions that reveal experience might include,

- What kinds of supports are the teachers who supervise the after-school tutoring session able to provide?
- Has the parent been supportive of the work you have undertaken with this child up to this point?

What is interesting about these questions is that they can be answered on a surface level, but they also serve as invitations to enter into discussion. While a couple of the questions above are not ideal, even if a teacher answered with yes or no, the coach could respond with a follow-up such as, "Tell me more about that." By using such questions and follow-up the coach can move the conversation beyond a surface-level response.

Questions Shaping Understanding. Questions that shape understanding can be extremely helpful to literacy coaches because in discussing students, teachers reveal a lot about their interpretive lens. Additionally, questions that shape understanding may provoke new thinking by teachers so that they are able to think on a deeper level and, therefore, obtain new insight into their own teaching. If literacy coaches pose questions that focus on connections, these questions might include

- What is the nature of the student writing in the language arts classroom versus the reading resource room?
- How did student engagement shift after you started to provide Keep Books to the child?
- What changes have you observed after the parents of students in your classroom completed your parent workshop?

Coaches pressing teachers to rethink or restate may use general prompts such as

- Tell me more about that.
- Why do you say that?

In other cases, more specific prompts might be used such as

- Can you tell me more about the way the student performance changed after reading his first Keep Book at home?
- Why did you describe some of the parents as overinvolved?

At other times, the literacy coach may prompt teachers to provide their point of view or demand an interpretation. This can be extremely helpful in better understanding the teacher's interpretive lens and, therefore, planning subsequent professional development sessions. These questions might include

- Why do you think "sound it out" is a helpful prompt for struggling students?
- Why do you think DIBELS is more useful than a running record?

We note that the characteristics of these sample questions include that they are largely nonjudgmental and that they can yield helpful information for both the coach and the teacher.

Questions Pressing for Reflection. Perhaps the most helpful set of questions are those that call for reflection. In some cases we may want teachers to develop a hypothesis of why things are the way they are. At times like this, we have sometimes defined *hypothesis* as an informed guess of the way the world works. In some cases, these hypotheses may be very large scale, and probes regarding the hypothesis may take place over months and years. This is especially the case if a teacher is conducting a study, perhaps as a part of a master's thesis or National Board certification. In these cases the coach may pose high-level probes to a teacher such as

- What is the nature of scaffolding at the point of difficulty?
- How can teachers be partnered within a critical friends approach to professional development?

In other cases, hypothetical questions might be much lower level and focused only on the events of a particular lesson. These might include

- Why does the student look at you when he reaches the end of a sentence?
- Why does the student read with his finger?

Like hypothetical questions, questions that focus on future action also can be posed that look at larger- and smaller-scale issues. Larger-scale future action questions might include

- What are goals for your teaching next year?
- How will you support daily reading when month-long proficiency tests are instituted next year?

Smaller-scale future action questions might include

- What will you change about your teaching in tomorrow's lesson to address the issues you just identified?
- How will you work with the resource room teacher this week to support this child in preparing for the test?

Finally, like hypothetical and future-action questions, questions that develop critical assessment also can operate on a larger and smaller plane but with a little bit of a twist. In some cases, the larger plane of critical assessment might be probes that are meant to prepare teachers not to talk about their teaching but to explain it to someone else. Larger-plane critical assessment questions might include

- Can you justify the expense of "safety net" teachers in your school?

- Can you explain the wisdom of having more than one teacher in a classroom?

In these cases, we might assume that the literacy coach is assisting teachers as they answer questions that might be posed by parents, community partners, benefactors, journalists, or administrators. In other cases, on a smaller plane, the coach may want to understand the teacher's critical assessment after new work was attempted or at the end of the year. These questions might include

- In what ways would you gauge the changes in your teaching after the first 6 months of coaching?
- Is the hard work we put in as a part of the coaching effort worth it?

Although Morgan and Saxton (1994) created their framework for teachers who pose questions for their students, their framework serves as a great gift for those of us who pose questions in a professional development setting. The complexity offered by the framework suggests that an important part of becoming a good literacy coach may indeed be to master the art of the question.

THE ART OF THE QUESTION

Certainly the work of Morgan and Saxton (1994) illustrates the astonishing complexity that goes into observing, creating a question based on the observation, and then asking the question. In fact, as many of us know, sometimes if we put just one or two words in the wrong place, we illicit a response quite different from what we sought. If we inadvertently select the wrong word, we might accidentally throw ourselves back into a judgmental, IRE response cycle. We also note that while the sample questions we posed above are largely nonjudgmental, many of them are quite difficult to answer. Therefore in this section we discuss preparing questions, using direct and less-direct questions, and supporting responses.

Preparing Questions

Clearly it is essential that because of the complexity of probing for understanding, questions receive careful attention from coaches. This is especially the case if a coach is trying to change an IRE pattern that has become established in the coaching, is working with a group of teachers new to him or her, is working with novice teachers, or is a first-time coach. To assist in the careful preparation of questions, we propose the following.

Advance Preparation. First, the coach should prepare questions in advance of the coaching session. Some questions might be global ones that are aligned with the purpose of the coaching session and others might be more specific. Especially for coaches who seek to master the art of the question, writing questions down will help to ensure that the wording avoids judgment, is specific, and capitalizes on some of the types of questions that we discussed above. Additionally, for those of us who have used Bloom's Taxonomy extensively, writing questions down is an opportunity to vary the level of complexity of the questions.

Examination of Questions. In preparing questions, a coach should give consideration to how direct those questions are. By *direct*, we mean the extent to which the question calls for an immediate and pressing response. For example, the question, Why did you do that? is extremely direct and may be viewed by some in certain contexts as hostile. A less-direct way of posing that question might be to ask, "Can you tell me about the decision making that led to your doing it that way?" In this case, the question is less direct because it appears to emphasize and honor the decision-making process of the teacher. Certainly we do not advocate more-direct questions over less-direct questions or vice versa. In fact, we have found in our work in the United States that the degree to which one can pose a more direct question is often a function of the geographic area of the country in which one works, the culture of the school or district, the nature of the relationship between coach and teachers, the background of the coach and teachers, and the personal affect of the coach (by this we mean that self-deprecating coaches adept at using humor can ask some pretty direct questions without causing offense).

We would certainly suggest that coaches consider all these factors as they prepare questions for teachers. It would also be interesting to hear from educators outside the U.S. setting and determine what factors shape how direct the coach is in creating a question. In the limited experiences we have in Commonwealth countries such as Australia, Canada, New Zealand, and the United Kingdom, we notice that the coaches seem to be much more direct in posing questions of teachers.

In addition to thinking about how direct a question is, coaches may wish to think during the preparation of their questions about whether they want to pose a question that demonstrates naked disagreement. Naked disagreement occurs when it is clear that the premise of the question disagrees with the thinking of the person to whom the question is posed.

For example, if a coach were to ask, "How do you reconcile your phonics approach in a classroom you say is based on whole language?" or "Yesterday you claimed you could help this student, but today you recommend he be pulled out and sent for special services. Which is it?" then we would have naked disagreement. Although naked disagreement questions are strident in tone, it may be that there are times when we have to ask the tough questions. In these cases we would suggest that the coach calculate the language of the question to gain understanding of the decision making rather than to expose weakness in the teacher's thinking. By understanding the decision making the coach may be better able to assist the teacher than he or she would by merely exposing weaknesses in the argument. In addition to resituating the purpose of the question, the coach can think about under what circumstances a question can be asked. Perhaps, for example, the question that poses the most naked disagreement might be discussed in private, thereby eliciting the most candid response.

Steps to Use in Asking Questions

We propose that coaches carefully consider how they ask their questions. In this section we suggest a sequence of steps that can be used in asking questions.

Stating the Role of Questions. One step is to state the role of questions in the coaching session. The coach might say at the beginning of an observation in which participants observe a teacher behind a one-way mirror:

> Today we're observing Aurora, and she asked for assistance on how she introduces a new book to the child. To help her I am going to ask you a lot of questions about what you are seeing her do, and then I will ask you more theoretical questions about how theory informs the teaching practice. In our debriefing session we can ask questions of each other about how practice informs theory and theory informs practice. It is important that we try to answer these questions so that we can help.

This short introduction accomplishes a lot. It tells teachers that answers to questions are not only expected but also needed to help Aurora. It creates anticipation by explaining that the coach will begin with lower-level observations; progress to intermediate-level remarks, explain the relationship between observation and theory; and conclude with a very high-level synthesis, in the debriefing, at which coach and teachers will ask questions of one another. Last, the introduction creates a stake for observation: Aurora has asked for our help.

Writing Questions Down. Another step that we would propose is that after the coach has introduced the lesson and explained the focus and role of questions, all participants, including the coach, write down their questions as the lesson unfolds. In this case, where teachers and coach are observing behind a one-way mirror, participants might ask these questions aloud. In other cases, where a coach is observing a live lesson, questions can be written to be used in later discussion. By writing questions during the lesson both coach and teachers have the opportunity to craft their questions. The coach can check his or her questions and revise them if necessary so that the questions are calculated to foster discussion and not agreement.

Waiting for Responses. Still another step that we think is essential is the careful use of wait time. Once a question has been posed by a teacher or the coach, let any awkward silence sit. Coaches should not take silence as a lack of engagement. Indeed, teachers may be highly engaged and working on an answer prior to speaking up. If a considerable amount of time has passed and no one has ventured a response, the coach may want to rethink the question and pose a different one. If we think about posing questions as a bid to recruit others into a conversation, it may be that the initial bid was too complex (or too simple!) and, therefore, a new bid is in order.

Since the most cognitively complex questions are likely to come in the debriefing, we would again suggest observing larger amounts of wait time here. We have also observed that some coaches ask highly useful, cognitively complex questions in the debriefing, but that teachers may respond on a much lower level. We think that this may be because they have just observed a lesson and therefore have a lot to say. As a result, there is a tendency to jump in and talk a lot while ignoring the highly crafted complex question that the coach has left on the table. We would propose that in the debriefing the coach start with a period in which the teachers just talk about the lesson. After this, the coach might begin with some of the higher-order questions.

Because the coach is asking higher-order questions it's unreasonable to expect instantaneous answers. Therefore we would suggest that the coach may want to write the most difficult questions, especially if they are multipart questions, on the board or overhead. In this way, teachers can attend to all parts of the question without fear of forgetting its parts. Additionally, we would propose that the coach provide time for teachers to think about some of the more difficult questions. An excellent way to do this is to write the question on the board and say something like, "This is an extremely difficult question. Let's take a few minutes to think about it and jot notes in our notebooks. Then we can share." In this way, the coach provides a time and a structure for thinking about the most difficult questions. If Vygotsky's (1978) claim that writing mediates thought is correct, providing time to jot notes may elicit a more in-depth response.

Seeking and Responding to Answers. A final step to consider is what we do after we have asked the question. When we pose extremely difficult questions, especially if the question is posed to an individual, there is a tendency from others to want to help the person out. Perhaps if the individual teacher does not answer, the coach will start to answer for the teacher. In other cases, other teachers may try to help out their colleague. As long as the coach can maintain a climate that feels like a coaching session and not an interrogation, we would advocate using techniques that ensure that the responsibility of answering the question is restricted to the person who was asked. To do this the coach must resist the urge to try to answer the question. Also, leveling eye contact at the person who was asked the question without outright staring that person down helps maintain the focus and precludes others from jumping in. Sometimes the teacher may literally look at others, which tends to draw them into the conversation. In this case, the coach may say, "Hang on there a second, Javier, I'd like to hear how Aurora answers this and then it would be interesting to see how you build on it." In using these techniques to restrict the responsibility for answering a difficult question to an individual, we are always amazed at the depth of response a teacher can generate. We have also learned to embrace the response "I don't know." We think that when teachers respond in this way, it is an indicator that they have reached the edge of their understanding. If we are truly trying to scaffold at the point of difficulty, this is a response that indicates we are going in the right direction.

Of course, there are times when a coach may ask a question of a teacher that is too difficult, poorly constructed, or perhaps even unanswerable! In that case, after sufficient wait time the coach might offer, "Aurora, it is a difficult question, and I have to tell you I don't really know how I'd answer it either. Let's write it down and think about it. Maybe we can talk about it later. In the meantime, Javier, what are you thinking?" Other variations of this include "It's a hard question, so can you think about it for a few minutes and we'll come back to you?" or "Maybe that question is too hard for any of us to answer right now. Something else we have discussed is . . ."

Another thing we should consider after we have asked the question is how the coach will respond to the teacher. From our own experiences as students many of us may remember how we felt about our own teachers saying, "Yes, but . . ." In this case we perhaps generated something we thought quite brilliant, received the apparently obligatory praise from the teacher, and then immediately had our work judged and characterized, with the message being that we had to go back to the drawing board. Indeed the judgment-negation or yes-but cycle is probably as damaging to dialogue as the IRE cycle. Thus, rather than affirming and negating, we would propose that the coach not judge at all. The coach needs to work at increasing the depth of understanding rather than appraising the worth of an initial understanding. Therefore instead of yes-but, the response is more likely to be "Can you tell me more about that?" or "Who else feels similarly?" or "What about the influence of . . . ?" A benefit of follow-up questions directed at seeking depth of response is that they move the conversation beyond ping-pong dialogue. By *ping-pong dialogue* we mean rapid-fire questions from the coach and answers from the teacher that cover only surface-level meaning. An emphasis on posing questions that elicit depth rather than coverage allows teachers to deliberate carefully and change their thinking as a result of the questions offered by a coach.

HOW COACHES HAVE DEVELOPED QUESTIONING

For the past several years Emily has worked with an international professional development initiative that uses both coaching training and an international network of coaches to support teachers in studying their work. As part of this effort Emily asked a number of coaches to reflect on their development of probing teacher understanding using questions. Their responses were interesting to us because they often overlapped with the principles that Morgan and Saxton (1994) described. Additionally, the coaches' responses informed our understanding of the art of the question. In the following section we describe the way in which coaches came to understand how questions could be used to probe understandings of teaching and learning. In the section that follows we describe how teachers can develop their own questions to support teacher ownership and agency, as well as build their own in-depth understanding of teaching and learning.

Coaches' Understandings of How to Use Questions

In this section we describe the reflections of three literacy coaches. The coaches all had years of successful teaching experience in the grades that they coached. All the coaches had at least a master's degree and a year of full-time university training in literacy coaching. Additionally, all taught children part time in the school district in which they coached, and they coached teachers part time using some of the strategies that we described in Chapter 5. Emily or her collaborators visited with these coaches as a follow-up to the university training, and it was at this time that the coaches reflected on their use of questions.

Asking Good Questions. In working with Lily, whom we introduced in Chapter 2, Emily concentrated on the nature of good questions:

> Emily talked with me after [my debriefing with teachers] about the kinds of questions that will foster discussion rather than the kind that will foster agreement with me. Questions that ask yes or no for answers almost always have the teacher thinking about what I must be thinking is the correct answer, rather than what the teacher needs to decide as the correct or more logical answer. Since debriefing is best when it is perceived as a conversation, I will add this to focus my discussions. Emily's idea of writing questions throughout the lesson observation will help me choose the best type of question for the areas of concern.

Internalizing Principles. We see an even better example of a coach beginning to internalize the principles around the art of asking questions in a reflection written by Maggie:

> One of the major goals I set for myself was to observe more and allow the teachers to gather evidence to discuss later. I did a better job observing. What helped the most was the discussion of the ping-pong discussion that was going on. Where I asked a question and someone answered, I clarified, someone else said something, I restated, etc. [I am beginning to] understand that we want the teachers to observe, build an understanding, look for evidence, observe, build an understanding, look for evidence, etc. This will cut back on the ping-ponging, and the teachers will interact while I lead them to their understandings that are grounded in the lesson and the observations. I need to ask myself, "How many times am I holding them accountable?" How often do I ask, "What is your evidence? Where do you see that?" or "What did you see that made you say that?" These types of questions are going to ground their understandings in the lesson that we are watching and give us all a common experience to talk about. It will also help

me continue to give appropriate observation time. Another big idea that we discussed afterward and in school visits is my pacing. I need to slow down, listen, construct my understandings, and not be afraid to slow down the pace, including how fast I talk.

In this reflection we can see that Maggie is making a powerful connection between what she observes in the lesson and how she can support enhanced observation by teachers. To support this effort she draws a link between what she observes and how she can use questions to hold teachers accountable for what they observe. In other words, her use of questions is a tool for summoning engagement by the teachers in the observation of the lesson. For Maggie, in addition to supporting engagement, the questions serve to ground teacher understandings both in the lesson and in theory. Finally, by slowing down to allow more time for careful thinking and the processing of ideas, Maggie feels she can support the co-construction of understanding with the teachers she coaches.

Using Notes. What is interesting about Maggie is that she uses notes in her observations of teachers not only to prepare questions, but also to capture what she observes for later use. In an earlier chapter we mentioned the use of scripting. In scripting the observer writes as rapidly as possible to try and capture the event being observed. In many cases a script will include extensive dialogue. The usefulness of the script is that the coach and teachers can turn to it later for a recounting of what occurred.

While scripts are one form of recording observational notes, there are other forms. In some cases coaches may begin an observation without taking any notes so that they are free to watch the lesson unfold. After a few minutes coaches may begin to focus on certain aspects of the teaching over others and then try to focus the notes around a particular component of the teaching. As the coaches' focus becomes clearer, they may intentionally try to write certain kinds of notes. In the sample notes below we have used standard abbreviations that we think most educators will understand. Types of notes include

1. *Hypothetical notes,* which contain observations that might assist the coach in building a hypothesis regarding teacher-student interaction or notes that might be of assistance to teachers in developing their own hypotheses. These notes might include comments such as "Stdt seems to prefer bks with female characters" or "Stdt extracts signif meaning from pictures."
2. *Procedural notes,* which document certain classroom procedures. These notes might include "Tchr spent 10 mins on attendance

in 3rd period" or "5 stdts spent 10 minutes finding their book" or "Jose never did get a pencil."

3. *Methodological notes* document the methodology of the coaching process and might include "Grt stdt wrk. Must bring camera" or "Want to video drama stdt wrk."

4. *Observational notes* record classroom events. Since this is the lesson log, they are likely to be bulleted in the following manner:

   - Stdts entered & went to centers.
   - T works with read-aloud center.
   - 3 stdts selct own bk. T helps 2 stdts select their bk.
   - T works with 1 child for 5 mins. Other child for 10 mins. Other kids on their own.
   - Child #1—Reads largely independently. T comments on features in pictures.

5. *Theoretical notes* are intended for further exploration whereby the coach can link the observation with coaching, literacy, or reading theory. These might include "How to explore if T instruction was within zpd [the zone of proximal development]?" or "What is link to Clay's hearing and recording sounds and words?"

There are other twists that coaches can put on this use of notes. Instead of categorizing the notes as they record them, coaches might take notes and then categorize them later. This approach might assist the coach in undertaking more powerful reflection based on the observation because there are tasks for the coach to complete after the lesson. An additional twist might be for a coach to observe a lesson with the explicit intent to only record one kind of note. For example, if a teacher was very advanced in his or her teaching, the coach might try to record only theoretical notes for the purpose of exploring high-level theory in the debriefing.

Stephanie's Use of Notes. In talking with Stephanie about her use of questions, we see a clearer picture of how coaches might use their notes. Like the previous two coaches, Stephanie discusses the importance of questions, but she also explains how she uses her notes to make for a more powerful debriefing:

Precise . . . language includes setting the stage before and summarizing afterward. In looking back at my notes . . . I can see the verbiage used to promote reflection and discussion of evidence among teachers: for example "What evidence do we have that . . . ?" and "Do you think . . . ?" followed by the ever popular "Why?" to open up discussion. My own language tended to be less open ended, and teachers often sat back and gave shorter answers that responded to my inquiries without delving into their own philosophy of teaching. Back in my training year, we were told that a particular list of questions was not developed because each [coach] needed to formulate questions based on the particular teacher and child before [him or her] at the moment. While I understand that theory, it is easier to formulate those questions for a continuing contact session when one has a higher-level example for reference. For me, the act of reviewing my scrawled . . . notes and transcribing them onto index cards was an exercise in deeper processing; I could see why some questions were much more likely to elicit multiple answers and deeper probing into teachers' thinking. The most powerful questions were started with, "Why?" "What else?" "What evidence?" and "Are you sure?" These gave teachers tacit permission to open up and theorize on the evidence before them as well as their own practices based on their theories.

In Stephanie's reflection we see an illustration of many of the concepts we have discussed earlier. There is, for example, the emphasis on setting the stage for observation followed by precise questioning. Stephanie also notes how she had to create more open-ended language to make the debriefing more accessible to teachers so that they did not sit back and give shorter answers. Most powerful of all, however, is how Stephanie is able to use her notes to deepen her own processing. In undertaking more theoretical work herself, she encourages the teachers she works with to do the same thing. Not only do they open up, they also engage in their own theory building. Obviously this is extremely powerful and it may be that the use of coded notes could further this work.

Developing Teachers' Understandings of How to Use Questions

Up to this point most of our attention has been directed to the use of questions by the literacy coach. This is problematic, because if teachers view the coach as the only person who can pose questions, they will inevitably feel that the coach owns the material, that they are being interrogated, and that the coach feels they have little to offer regarding teaching and learning. Therefore it is essential that coaches think carefully about how they can support the development and ownership of questions posed by teachers.

What Not to Do and Why Not to Do It. When we started out as college instructors we perhaps naively assumed that we could provide owner-ship for our college-level students by telling them to ask more questions. Adrian can remember one graduate class that went something like this:

> ADRIAN: I have been thinking about my teaching and realized the other day that I have been asking all the questions. I decided you should have a time when you could ask questions of me. So what questions do you have?
>
> STUDENTS: [Silence.]
>
> ADRIAN: [Uses wait time—silence.]
>
> STUDENTS: [More silence.]
>
> ADRIAN: OK, I can see that this is a difficult question. Let's take a few minutes to jot down some questions so we can talk about them. [Five minutes pass. Little has been written down.]
>
> ADRIAN: Great. What questions have you come up with?
>
> STUDENT: How long is the term paper again?

After such a painful experience, that's something Adrian did not want to repeat again! It would be easy to lapse back into "owning the rite of asking questions" but Freire (1993) helps us out here by thinking about teacher ownership and agency. He explained that ownership can-not exist when it is given. Thus when Adrian said, "I decided you should ask more questions," he really had just reasserted his right to decide when and where the questions get asked. Freire also explains that when students have been oppressed for a long time, they will continue to work from within the limits of their oppression even when they have more freedom. Since Adrian had not given the students the opportunity to ask questions at any previous point, the students would not now suddenly clamor to be heard, with lists of questions. Instead it is more likely that the students would wait until the social order that had been established restored itself.

Creating a Venue for Teacher Questions. Given that much of preser-vice and inservice education is dominated by the instructor asking the questions and the teachers providing the answers, and given that the one-shot workshop features a so-called expert who will tell teachers ev-erything they need to know in 2 hours, the state of teacher preparation and professional development does not bode well for building owner-ship by teachers over questions. Even Freire (1993), who writes about liberatory pedagogy, would seem to think that those of us interested in change agentry have our work cut out for us because teachers who are asked for input will often respond in the way we taught them. Therefore we propose that we need to build the capacity for teacher ownership over questions.

One venue in which coaches can build such capacity is at whole-group meetings. Small-group cluster visits are often targeted and the coach may not want to give up a lot of the question-posing responsibility to teachers who are in the fledgling stages of developing their own questions. The whole-group meeting may provide more latitude for teachers to construct their own questions. Of course the difficulty with a large group is that teachers will be reluctant to pose a question in front of 20 or 30 colleagues. The coach may want to divide the whole group into smaller groups, possibly based on areas of interest. In these special interest groups, teachers might pose questions of one another. In the coach's effort to provoke questions of deeper and high complexity, the coach might recommend that questions that cannot be answered in the small group be brought back to the whole group for further discussion and analysis. In this way, the teacher who posed the original question has the small group agreeing that the question is worthy of analysis by the entire group. Additionally, teachers can have the experience of having their questions move from the more private analysis of the small group to the more public analysis of the whole group. Finally, by bringing teachers' questions to the whole group for consideration, the coach has the possibility of using the questions to seed potential case studies.

Redefining Inquiry and Teacher Ownership. One of the difficulties of partnering with teachers is that coaches tend to take on the responsibility for focusing the inquiry. As a result the coaching enterprise can easily be dominated by the coach with little role for the teachers. The development of case studies within a coaching context provides for greater ownership over who owns the questions and who will be engaged in finding answers.

Of course the difficulty with case studies is that some teachers may regard them as extra work, above and beyond the work of the coaching enterprise. It is important that coaches who are thinking about asking teachers to develop case studies consider how motivated a teacher is to conduct inquiry into a question and what audience might exist with whom the teacher can share the results of this inquiry. Certainly a case study might begin as a small-scale initiative whereby the results are meant to be shared only with other teachers in the coaching network by way of poster sessions at the end of the year. Perhaps in some cases teachers who become very interested in their case study may be able to use it with other audiences. These might include using their case in a National Board portfolio or a master's exit portfolio or as a conference presentation at a regional or national conference such as those sponsored by IRA or NCTE. Clearly this would be quite ambitious work in the beginning years of establishing a coaching network, but

> teacher ownership dramatically changes the way teacher education research can be represented. In the future, teams of teachers and researchers will need to study what happens when they mutually construct research questions, when they overlap teaching and researching responsibilities, and when they consider multiple ways of representing data. (A. Rodgers, 2002, p. 156)

Coaches and teachers working together offer the possibility that the education profession can begin building that future of practitioner and researcher co-constructed inquiry today. In doing so, we can move from the efforts we described above that are directed at building the capacity for teacher questions to a day when teachers pose the questions created as a part of coaching sessions.

Dramatic Ways to Support Teacher Questions. Up to this point we have considered somewhat traditional ways to think about how coaches can support teachers in posing questions. There are also some nontraditional methods coaches can use, and these include *hot seating* and *working in-role*. The use of the hot-seating technique is quite dynamic and often results in a high degree of engagement by the participants. As one can surmise from the name, the hot seat forces a teacher to face uncomfortable questions and respond to them. The purpose of using hot seating in the coaching context is that different kinds of responses can be attempted by the teacher in the safety of the coaching context so that when a similar event occurs on the job, the teacher feels prepared to deal with the issue. When working in-role, one or more participants takes on the persona of another individual. Sometimes this individual is a fictional generic character, such as an "angry parent" or a "petulant politician"; other times the in-role work is based on an as-if character. In these cases a participant might be asked to work in-role as if he or she were another teacher who had just been asked to cover the fifth class for a teacher in a coaching initiative.

Let's imagine a scenario where a teacher has requested assistance with a parent he or she perceives as challenging. The parent, a single mother and successful attorney at a large law firm, is upset about her child's scores on a recent teacher-made test and has requested a meeting with the teacher. Prior to the meeting the parent has sent a note on her law office's letterhead to the teacher that reads:

15 May 2007

Dear Ms. Granillo,

You and I both know that Maria is a much better student than the C you gave her on her test. On her paper you wrote, "Work harder at providing reasons for what you say." I do not agree with your claim that Maria fails to provide sufficient evidence for her ideas.

I am sure we can come to an agreement about this issue when we meet. I look forward to our meeting at 3:50 Tuesday. I will have 25 minutes available to meet with you.

Sincerely,
Maura Rodrigues, J.D.
(Maria's mom)

The day prior to the meeting the teacher meets in a whole-group session with her coach and fellow teachers and requests assistance. In the prebriefing to the hot seating, the teacher shares the letter and explains she is nervous about the meeting for a number of reasons: She has never received a parent note on letterhead; she perceives the tone of the note to challenge a professional decision; she is concerned the meeting will be contentious; she wants to work with the parent but feels the parent wants to work against her; she is concerned that issues may be raised that cannot be adequately dealt with in the time the parent has; and she feels uncomfortable about the social status the parent has adopted—a feeling exacerbated by the legalistic nature of the letter.

On the basis of this prebriefing, the coach asks the teachers to pose questions that might be similar to the ones that Ms. Rodrigues will ask. Most important, the coach suggests to the teacher in the hot seat that she work hard to take any question posed by Ms. Rodrigues and respond by talking about Maria's reading and writing. In this way, the coach explains, the parent meeting can be about Maria, and the teacher can work with the parent on problem solving.

As the hot seating gets under way and fellow teachers call out questions that sound very much like what we might anticipate Ms. Rodrigues would ask, the teacher in the hot seat has a meltdown. Her responses go awry, and it is clear this could be a contentious meeting! Fortunately, because of the hot-seating technique, the teacher-observers can suggest alternate responses, the coach can restart the session, and the teacher can practice her responses to prepare for the dreaded meeting.

In a variation on the hot-seating technique, some or all of the participants can work in-role. For example, after the teacher has become comfortable with her responses in the hot seat, the coach might enter a mock meeting, taking the part of Ms. Rodrigues. Using the in-role technique, the coach poses the same questions that were asked by the observer-teachers earlier. This has a more intense effect and may be more representative of what the teacher will experience. Again, the emphasis of the coach is on supporting the teacher in steering questions so that the parent and teacher can discuss Maria's reading and writing.

Emily has used the hot-seating and in-role techniques extensively. We see these techniques as being especially useful when teachers are called on to help promote the concept of literacy coaching. This promotion of literacy coaching includes speaking to teachers not currently being coached, addressing administrators at district-level meetings, and meeting with politicians at social and formal events such as school board meetings. What is important about these contexts is that hot-seating and in-role work provide an opportunity for all teachers to pose highly politicized questions; practice answers; and take a greater role in the political agency that increasingly surrounds the teaching of reading, writing, speaking, and listening.

CONCLUSION

In this chapter we used a framework developed by Morgan and Saxton (1994) to think about how coaches could observe teaching, devise questions, pose questions, and solicit responses from teachers. We also explained that it is essential that coaches support teachers in empowering themselves by providing opportunities to pose and respond to questions in contentious contexts. The ability to reflect and respond deeply to a probe by a fellow teacher, coach, administrator, or community member is becoming more and more important in the so-called era of accountability that grips American educational culture at the beginning of the 21st century.

Increasingly, educators can expect to have their professional knowledge questioned by more and more constituents using an array of tools calculated to measure and deconstruct what teachers do. As a result, it is essential that if the difficult but quality work that can grow out of coaching is to be maintained and supported despite increasing challenges from the system, participants in coaching networks need to be able to demonstrate how they used coaching to devise answers to tough questions about teaching and learning.

CHAPTER 9

One Coach, One Teacher: Getting the Most Out of Working One to One

with Mary Fried

In Chapter 2 we described a continuum of support that a coach might offer to a teacher: from less intense activities such as planning lessons and finding materials, to more intense activities such as supporting reflection about teaching (see Bean, 2004a; Rodgers & Pinnell, 2002). A coach may visit a teacher at school for any of these activities, but in this chapter we will focus solely on the kind of school visit that is intended to support reflection and scaffold teacher change. This is the most intense kind of coaching because it involves an observation of teaching followed by discussion with the teacher. The challenge is to go beyond surface-level niceties, to coach reflection and inquiry, and to create change in teaching and student learning. Coaches can do this by creating a collaborative context in which analysis and reflection are encouraged and supported.

Each of us has been the coach in that situation and has also observed and given feedback to coaches on school visits. In this chapter we draw from our experiences and from the implications of our own case study research to share what we have learned about the nature of effective school visits. We discuss issues such as gathering information before the observation, deciding if and when to offer help, and mining examples from the observation to use in the discussion afterward. We also present a case scenario from a school visit to illustrate how effective coaches foster genuine conversations to engage the teachers in reflection and problem solving. We begin first with a timely reminder about the promise of professional development.

SCHOOL VISITS:
CONNECTING ACTION AND PRACTICAL KNOWLEDGE

Richardson's (1996) literature review about the role that attitudes, beliefs, and experiences play in learning to teach extends both a promise and challenge for literacy coaches. According to her review, it is probably easier to change inservice teachers' beliefs about teaching than it is to change the beliefs of preservice teachers. She attributes this difference to the fact that inservice teachers have the benefit of experiences; no doubt these experiences support their reflection and thinking about teaching, and that makes it more likely that they might change how they teach. Without this rich backdrop of teaching experiences, preservice teachers have only their experiences as students to inform their views on teaching.

Richardson's (1996) conclusion is especially instructive, and this is where we find both the promise and challenge for literacy coaches. She said, "The deep practical knowledge held by experienced teachers is closely tied to action, and it is this action that is understood by teachers to be the focus of change" (p. 114). We think this information about the potency of action to influence practical knowledge is good news for literacy coaches. It underscores the potential of teaching experiences to have a profound impact on practice, but by the same token extends the challenge to literacy coaches to ground their coaching in real teaching experiences. As we already know, coaching reflection around teaching is one of the most intense forms of professional development.

Adrian noted the power of grounded professional development as a vehicle for change in his discussion of professional development formats for inservice teachers (A. Rodgers, 2002). As well, Sprinthall et al. (1996) reviewed three major studies and identified elements of an effective teacher education program. Teacher education programs, they said, should be embedded in a school context and be purposeful and articulated. The relationship between the staff developer and teacher should be participatory and collaborative, with an emphasis on knowledge building, analysis, and reflection. Finally, the professional development should be ongoing and developmental in nature, acknowledging that teachers will be building necessary background knowledge of theory and research as the program of professional development progresses.

We think that the school visit, as a format for professional development, holds great potential to change teaching because it contains all of the elements of effective teacher education as identified by research. The coach, having observed the teacher teach, has a shared experience with the teacher, which can ground the coach's analysis and inquiry afterward. After the teaching, either the coach or the teacher can work with students to trial an instructional procedure, providing the setting for a participatory and collaborative relationship where theories are tested as well as fostering reflection so that the process moves along. By its very nature the school visit is embedded within the school context, not decontextualized, as so many professional development sessions become when they are held in a hotel conference room by a presenter who stands and delivers information. The school visit, as a format for professional development, certainly appears to hold great potential to support teacher change.

BEFORE THE TEACHING

We have found that the most important work that a coach can do to help ensure the success of a school visit takes place well before the visit. After all, as we learned in Chapter 3, we know that anxiety and fear can have a serious impact on a person's ability to learn. Certainly, preparing for a school visit in which the coach will observe the teacher teach will likely cause some worry and apprehension for any teacher. Planning ahead not only will help the visit go well but also may reduce the teacher's anxiety. This means that teachers should know in advance of the visit:

- Why the coach is coming to visit them
- When the visit will take place
- What the coach expects to see and do
- Approximately how long the visit will last
- What the teacher needs to do to prepare

Setting the Purpose of the School Visit

Because the most powerful changes in teaching can be accomplished as a result of the school visit, it is important that the coach and the teacher determine in advance what the purpose of the school visit is to be. This can be decided in a number of ways. One possibility is that the teacher has requested the coach come to the school because the teacher seeks feedback on a particular component of teaching. Another possibility is that the coach has determined that all the teachers in the coaching network need support with a particular aspect of their teaching. Yet another possibility is that in whole-group meetings of the coaching network, the teachers have divided themselves into special interest groups. Since the teachers in each special interest group are focusing on a particular component of their teaching, the coach might decide to visit each teacher to support the latter's focused approach.

Regardless of which circumstances brought about the coaching visit, much more work must be undertaken prior to the meeting. The coach should talk with the teacher, or at the very least be in e-mail contact, so that the focus of the observation can be discussed. In some cases a teacher might share a lesson plan with a coach. In other cases the teacher may share evaluations of a student with a coach for the purpose of obtaining feedback so as to best help the child. Still in other cases it may be that the coach and teacher hold frequent discussions around some aspect of teaching in the whole-group meeting, and the purpose of the visit is to inform these discussions. Considerable discussion to decide the focus of the visit must take place before the event is scheduled.

The Coach's Purpose. In our experience, literacy coaches usually have backgrounds as very successful teachers. As former successful teachers with good practical knowledge about teaching children, coaches may be tempted to focus their energy on helping students on school visits. A large part of this desire may come from their enjoyment of the experience of teaching children and a scarcity of opportunities to do so since their becoming coaches. Coaches also often have a deep commitment to help students learn, and it's this commitment that makes it difficult for them not to focus on students—particularly if they know they can easily make a difference in their learning. As such, coaches can mistakenly gear their work to shifting student participation and understanding rather than shifting teacher practice and understanding.

The more generative and powerful work of a school visit will come in creating shifts in teaching that will potentially have a far greater impact on more students. To help maintain this focus, we coach coaches to think about this question: What support can you provide that will make the greatest difference in teaching? There may be more than one thing to work on, but this question at least directs the coach's attention to teaching rather than to the students. The way into this analysis and reflection on teaching will be through the student's work (as we discuss in Chapter 4 in our description of collaborative inquiry), but the goal is to change teaching practice.

The Teacher's Purpose. The purpose of a coaching visit is always to support the teacher in working on teaching. Just as the coach must know the purpose of visiting a teacher, it is essential that the teacher also have a purpose for the visit. The teacher may want to think about this in advance and be able to share these goals with the coach. Thus it is important that the teacher be free to undertake this difficult work. The teacher should not schedule a visit during a testing period, extremely late in the school year, or at a time when there are a number of personal issues to which that teacher must attend.

In addition to having a general purpose, the teacher should be able to articulate more specific goals. We have learned that even one apparently unassuming goal set by a teacher can have a number of important characteristics. Imagine that a teacher is talking to a coach and says, "I need feedback on the level and kind of support I provide to students during guided reading." The characteristics of this request are the following:

- It is specific to the guided reading part of the lesson.
- It articulates the level of support offered to the students as one of the foci.
- It is a nuanced statement because the teacher looks not only at the amount of support, but also at the kind of support.
- It is apparent that the teacher has a genuine interest in knowing more about this part of the teaching.
- It is something that is within the power of the teacher to change.
- It is reasonable to believe that one observation of a lesson could provide the coach with sufficient information so that the coach can at least begin to respond to this request for assistance.
- It is reasonable to believe that a question about the amount and kind of help is within the coach's expertise.
- It is theoretically grounded in the work of Vygotsky, Bruner, and Clay.

When creating goals for classroom visits, teachers might want to make short, crisp statements that have some of the features we identified above. Before the lesson, coaches should specifically ask teachers what feedback they want on their teaching and make sure they are thinking and talking about their teaching, not the child's responding. Coaches who encounter teachers who articulate goals like "Everything" or "My teaching prompts" will need to get the teachers to be more specific. This could be the first time teachers have really thought about how the teaching is going, and they may need the guidance of the coach to help them articulate goals. The objective in creating a goal statement is to help teachers become as thoughtful and analytical about their teaching as they are about the students' learning.

One of the most difficult things in scheduling the visit is to resist the urge to create a "show lesson" in which teachers show off the best, surefire material. In fact, in working with coaches, the most powerful work comes when teachers are working at the edge of their knowledge or are trying to do something extremely difficult or new. Perhaps a part of the reason teachers are tempted to produce show lessons is because they want their professional practices to be held in high regard. For this reason, we think it is essential that teachers first invite coaches, not necessarily to a show lesson, but to a lesson or a part of a lesson with a class that is likely to go well. Coaches might take special interest in observing a part of a lesson that teachers feel particularly confident about and in which they do not need a lot of feedback.

Some might think that our rationale here would be to create a positive experience for teachers where the stakes are low. That's true—and even important, given what we know about the role of emotions in learning—but our primary reason is a little different. We think that before coaches begin to problem-solve with teachers around tricky cases, it is vital to see the teaching going well so that impressions of teaching are not skewed. Another benefit of observing the teaching going well is that coaches will be knowledgeable about the teachers' strengths and use that information to build on during the next visit when they need to problem-solve together. In this way, teacher and coach can build confidence and trust in one another. Importantly, teachers can be assured that coaches know they can do great teaching so that they are freed to subsequently share the more challenging work with an outsider on later visits.

Scheduling the Visit

It is essential that teachers know when the coaching visit is going to occur. Even if coaches and teachers already share a fabulous collegial relationship, they will not be collaborators for long if the coach makes a habit of popping in for a surprise visit. The teachers will no doubt think that coaches are deliberately trying to catch teachers off guard, placing teachers in the worst possible light. Certainly coaches would have a difficult time making the case that they are there to support teachers. The role of coaches becomes one of evaluator and supervisor in such a case, and we think this is a serious distortion of the coaches' role. Of course, it is quite different if teachers request a coaching visit sooner than a regularly scheduled visit. Since many teachers may want support in analyzing their teaching, they should know that they have this option.

Ample time should be set aside for the school visit so that the coach can talk briefly with the teacher before the observation, observe the teaching, and then have enough time to thoroughly debrief afterward. In many contexts 90 minutes to accomplish these three tasks is a useful guideline. An hour is just not enough time to do the complex work of shifting the teacher's understandings and observing the lesson. It may seem easier to schedule the debriefing for another day, given the investment of time already given to observing the teaching, but it is important to connect the debriefing with the observation while examples are still fresh.

The structure of the school visit means that the teacher needs to be prepared to alter the usual day's schedule in order to accommodate the planned work. Because there may have to be changes in the teaching schedule in order to accommodate the coach's school visit, it is important that the teacher seek the assistance of other teachers. The changes in schedule go beyond being available when the coach arrives at the school. It may be that a student or students would be asked to come back a second time to work with the teacher and coach to try out theories that were developed as a result of the lesson debriefing. Often the coach may want to demonstrate a few teaching procedures that were described to the teacher. In these cases it is important that a teacher have communicated potential schedule changes to fellow teachers so that the timetable alterations can be accommodated. Their ability to make the necessary changes to their schedules assists the teacher in being able to take full advantage of the powerful learning experience offered by a coaching visit.

Deciding What Teaching to Observe

Teachers should know beforehand what the coach expects to see during the school visit. We are referring here to a plan for observation as specific as teaching a guided reading lesson to third-grade students or teaching eighth-grade students how to peer-edit. The decision about what to observe will be straightforward in cases in which teachers have requested support on some particular aspect of their teaching, but even then both teacher and coach should be specific.

The literacy coach will also want to schedule and set the focus for school visits depending on the coach's ongoing work. For example, the coach may want to follow up on a previous school visit in which he or she worked with a teacher to analyze a specific part of the literacy lesson together and set goals for shifts in teaching. After a few weeks of working on these goals, with opportunity for reflection, the teacher may have follow-up questions and new ideas about the teaching that the coach can help fine-tune with a second visit. In other cases, the coach may want to schedule school visits to individual teachers following the introduction of new ideas in a whole-group professional development setting. These teachers may need additional support or they may simply want continuing contact with the coach just to have feedback while trialing the new ideas.

Coaches will also make decisions on what they want to see and do on a school visit based on their ongoing monitoring of how teachers and students are progressing. Many coaches with whom we have worked collect monthly reports or updates from teachers about how things are going. Teachers might write a brief, anecdotal report on how things are going and identify an issue or question for follow-up with the coach. If similar issues or questions arise across the anecdotal reports, the coach could decide to do a series of school visits to target the common challenges that teachers are experiencing with their teaching.

How the coach operates within a building or district is likely to be shaped by the needs of the school or the system, as well as the opportunities allotted within existing contracts the district may have with its teachers. An additional factor is how the district and the coach define the description of the coaching position.

Certainly there are a number of issues that will need to be addressed when hiring the literacy coach. The degree of autonomy of the coach, how much time the coach spends with teachers, and which teachers are identified to be coached are all a part of the decision making that will need to occur between the employer and the prospective coach.

Setting the Focus for the Observation

The observation begins with a preconferencing session that is usually held just before the observation. It is critical at this time that the coach be most respectful of the teacher and the classroom. Many coaches are not staff members of the school, and therefore, they are guests. Thus it is essential that the coach observe any local customs to avoid alienating staff and students. Certainly there are a number of them, from sign-in and sign-out procedures to wearing identification, so it is important that the coach arrive in sufficient time to negotiate the niceties prior to undertaking the prebriefing.

During the prebriefing the coach might review notes from the last visit, review teaching goals from the last visit to determine if they have changed, and briefly gather other information prior to the lesson. It can be extremely valuable at this time to gather student information by discussing students with the teacher and reviewing evaluations of the students conducted by the teacher. We have already discussed the importance of "teaching today's child"; the coach should note whether the student work under review is current. In lower grades in which teachers use a leveled-book approach, the coach might check on the distribution of students to the leveled groups and whether students are able to make their way from one level to the next. This is also a good time for the coach to remind the teacher that the coach might interrupt with either side coaching or a demonstration. If this occurs the teacher can observe and take notes.

During the prebriefing many literacy coaches ask questions, including

- What are the strengths of the students?
- What are the biggest problems faced by the students?
- What supports do the students need so they can learn at the instructional level?
- What can students do independently?
- What is the teacher working on in the teaching?
- Is there anything special the teacher wants the coach to look for?

We would pose three caveats about asking these questions. The first is that the coach should pay special attention to the teacher's response to the first question. In our coaching experience we notice that teachers frequently focus on what the student cannot do; often when discussing strengths teachers lapse into talking about weaknesses of the student. The second caveat is that it is important that the coach not try to do too much problem solving until after the lesson. Extensive analysis of student records at this point may lead the coach down the wrong road, be time consuming, and be unproductive. Most important, the coach may be blinded from pursuing more fruitful outcomes. The third caveat is that the coach should try to limit the prebriefing to about 10 minutes. When 10 minutes are exceeded there is a tendency to engage in too much analysis.

DURING THE TEACHING

Once the observation begins, the coach can use a number of techniques. Many of the coaches we have worked with often begin by scanning the room, sometimes moving about to gather information. In the initial review of the room the coach observes the environment, looking at the use of centers; the size and suitability of chairs, tables, and spaces; the word wall; the accessibility of the room for the students; the presence of student work in the room; the presence of student writing portfolios that support the opportunity for students to write in different genres; and the presence of books that are easy enough to be read independently by all children.

During this very early phase of the observation the coach might also identify a good location from which to observe the teaching, attending to such features as accessibility for moving around the room and being close enough to observe student activity. It is important in tutorial settings such as small group, shared reading, and one-to-one work that the coach sit just behind and next to the student so that the coach can observe the child's behaviors from the same perspective as the child. At times like this the coach should never sit across the table. Additionally, the very beginning of the observation is an opportunity to greet and interact with the student. It is important that the student knows why the coach is there; we have found the most powerful greeting that works with any age to be "I am visiting your class today so I can learn to be a better teacher. Will you help me be a better teacher?"

Once the teacher begins the lesson the coach has a number of options. Two options that we have already discussed are the use of scripting (Chapter 4) and the use of coded notes (Chapter 8). A third option includes selective scripting, in which the coach divides the page into two columns. The coach uses one column to script selected parts of the lesson related to the focus of the observation. These scripted interactions provide specific examples of what happened that the coach and teacher can return to later during the debriefing. The other column provides a place for the coach to write "notes to self." These may be questions that arise as the coach observes the teaching that he or she plans to pose later. The coach might also write analytical notes to self that will support the debriefing.

Regardless of what note form is used, systematic notes assist in organizing observations during the lesson, setting goals for teacher shifts, and revisiting observations and teacher goals on subsequent school visits. Since we will be recommending a time limit for the debriefing, notes also assist the coach in prioritizing the most important components of the lesson to discuss in the debriefing. We have found that the limited time available for the debriefing permits a discussion of a maximum of two major issues and a couple of minor procedural ones. Indeed, sometimes if a more pressing issue arises during the observation, such as one related to student safety, the coach may decide to discuss this rather than one of the stated goals of the lesson. Therefore notes serve to prioritize what is to be discussed after the observation and what can be saved for discussion on a different day.

Using Rubrics to Focus Observation but Not Evaluate Teaching

One of the difficulties of using the selective-scripting or the coded-notes methods of recording observations is the problem of what to record. In Chapter 4 we described a research project in which observational rubrics were developed to support the work of literacy coaches. The rubrics contained elements that went beyond the teaching to deal with the classroom itself—how it was set up and how students worked together and interacted with the teacher. It was felt that coaches needed to observe and think about more than teaching in order to gain insight about instruction and to be able to give the teacher robust feedback and support. We have not provided those rubrics in this book because we think that it is important that coaches develop their own rubrics about what they are looking for and the degree to which the teacher and classroom exemplify that. Ideally, rubrics are developed with the input of teachers so that the rubrics are relevant to each coaching and teaching context.

To support coaches and teachers on getting started with the development of rubrics, we can explain that our rubrics were divided into teaching and nonteaching elements. The nonteaching elements included

- Classroom materials and organization
- Student engagement
- Quality of interactions
- Sense of community

When we considered classroom organization, we identified four levels of degree:

- Materials are not organized; it is almost impossible to quickly find or distribute materials.
- Some materials are organized for efficient use by the teacher and students.
- Most materials are organized for efficient use by the teacher and students.
- Materials are highly organized for efficient use by the teacher and students.

When we considered sense of community, we identified these four levels of degree:

- There is little or no evidence that the teacher helps students to take responsibility for their own behavior and learning and to demonstrate respect for the learning of others. Teacher controls interaction of students.
- The teacher helps students to take some responsibility for their own behavior and learning and to demonstrate respect for the learning of others some of the time.
- The teacher helps students to take responsibility for their own behavior and learning and to show respect for the learning of others most of the time.

- The teacher helps students to take a high degree of responsibility for their own behavior and learning and to show respect for the learning of others (e.g., students know routines and why they use them; they help and treat others with respect).

Although it will take time for coaches and teachers to work together to develop rubrics, the activity can be a worthwhile one. If coaches and teachers can accept that the purpose of the rubric is not to level judgment or to evaluate and rate teachers and teaching, the participants will be free to use the rubric as a springboard for discussing how we look at teaching.

Opportunities for Side Coaching and Demonstrating

In Chapter 5 we explained that if a coach was to use side coaching, it needed to be decided in advance, highly directive, brief, and infrequent in occurrence. Another option for the coach during the observation is to interrupt the teaching to provide a demonstration. A demonstration is different from side coaching in that the coach actually stops the teacher from teaching and steps into the teacher role. Of course, we remind coaches that since their job is to support the professional growth of the teacher rather than the educational growth of the child, the coach must limit interactions with students. The timing of the demonstration is critical so as not to make the lesson too disjointed. In our experience demonstrations can be offered at four points:

- The end of a component of the lesson (The coach could select any component early, midway, or late in the lesson and demonstrate at that point.)
- The end of the lesson (This is so the coach can go back to any component of the lesson sequence.)
- After the debriefing (At this time the teacher or coach can have the student return so that the coach can demonstrate a specific interaction.)
- After the visit (A coach may decide to schedule a follow-up visit to provide demonstration and the opportunity for additional coaching.)

By using strategies that include careful observation, note taking, rubric use, and side coaching or demonstrating, both coach and teacher should be fully prepared for a robust debriefing.

DEBRIEFING AFTER TEACHING

The coach must work very hard to constrain the debriefing to a maximum of 25 minutes (not counting the time it might take to go and get students for the purpose of demonstrating a technique). Since the purpose of the debriefing is to deliver robust coaching that features high degrees of engagement from both participants, the goal is to have a riveting 20 or 25 minutes rather than a mediocre 1-hour talk. In fact we even know one coach who uses a timer as a part of her debriefings!

Using the Debriefing to Create Powerful Learning

The exigency of time means that coaches will have to restrict their comments to a maximum of two big issues and perhaps a couple of small procedural ones. At the same time they are seeking a breakthrough so that they can support teachers in changing their teaching. To accomplish this, coaches have a number of options.

Debriefing Options. There is no set sequence for the debriefing, but options include

- Discussing each side coaching event
- Returning to the goals stated at the beginning of the lesson
- Returning to a demonstration offered during the lesson
- Involving the teacher in planning for a demonstration that could be modeled in the debriefing

The debriefing provides an excellent opportunity for the coach to refer to guidebooks that might be offered by programs that are in use in the school, use demonstration, perform role plays, and clarify procedures that inform teaching points. Since no one understands complex activity just by talking about it, it is important that procedures and prompts be seen and practiced.

Additionally, it is essential that during the debriefing coaches work to guide teachers to an analysis of their own decisions in relation to both the students' strengths and what the students need to learn. This is a time when coaches need to be ready to help teachers problem-solve for students who are making very slow progress. In some cases, if teachers and coaches are unable to make progress during the debriefing, coaches may opt to call in an additional coach or a teacher who may have experienced success with similar students as a part of a future visit.

Creating Powerful Learning. The goal for all school visits is to help teachers gain a higher, independent level of understanding that will result in accelerated learning for all their students. We are always amazed at how coaches are able to do this. To provide you with an example of what is possible, let's describe a case of a coach debriefing with a teacher whom Emily observed.

Emily observed a lesson in which a coach was working with a teacher in a tutoring session with one student who was behind his peers in his reading ability. As a part of this lesson the teacher and coach agreed that the student should reread some familiar books to develop good phrasing and fluency. The teacher in our example chose two familiar lessons for the student to reread, but one book turned out to be too hard for the student. In the following exchange, which depicts a debriefing session, the task of the coach is to support the teacher in realizing that while her scaffolding might have been good, it was focused on helping the student problem-solve new words and not on teaching the student to read in a phrased way.

COACH: How did things go with the two familiar books?
TEACHER: He's doing well. He read word by word, though, especially in the new book.
COACH: Well, he might not be as fluent reading the new book because it's not familiar, so he has a bit more solving to do. How did he sound on familiar reading?
TEACHER: Better on the first book, but that was more familiar to him.
COACH: Was there a difference in teaching, too?
TEACHER: I helped him solve more words on the second book. I guess I did more teaching on that one.
COACH: Yes, I think so too.
TEACHER: He was having difficulty on the second book so I jumped in a lot. I guess I shouldn't do that during familiar rereading.
COACH: Why not?
TEACHER: He's supposed to be learning how to read in a phrased and fluent way. So if I did any teaching it should probably be about phrasing. Hmm, so that second book may have been too hard to use for familiar reading.

In this example we can see that the coach does a nice job of supporting the teacher in self-diagnosing her work. One of the reasons that the coach does not simply tell the teacher to use an easier book is because then the learning would be about this child and this lesson. By supporting the teacher in reflecting on her practice and understanding her own teaching, the coach is supporting long-term change.

Wrapping Up the Debriefing

At the end of the debriefing the coach should focus on what has been learned as a result of the observation and wrap up the visit. The teacher should also be able to summarize new learning and insights from the coaching visit and to set goals based on this visit for future teaching with other students.

The final step in the debriefing is to plan subsequent activity. This might include scheduling a follow-up visit to work on issues identified in the observation that could not be explored during the debriefing. Not every visit should have an immediate follow-up, so the job of the coach is to determine under what circumstances follow-up visits should be scheduled.

It is difficult to know how many times a year a coach should conduct a school visit to a teacher. On the one hand, a couple of times a semester sounds about right to support teacher progress over the course of a year. For a coach who teaches a half day in a school and coaches the remainder of the day, that may be quite reasonable. On the other hand, some of the coaches we know provide professional development to nearly 40 teachers. At six visits a year, that would be 240 visits for an instructional year that lasts only 180 days!

The job of each coach is to balance the geographic area served, the number of teachers, the number of school visits, the number of cluster visits, the number of small-group meetings, and the number of whole-group meetings so as to create a coaching plan that is robust but makes sense. In creating this optimal plan the coach must also consider how observations will be conducted. Depending on what the coach and teacher are working on, a coach might schedule a visit that permits the observation of two lessons with two different groups of students or a visit that entails observation of 20 minutes of one lesson with a return the following day to observe another 20-minute component of a lesson.

POSTDEBRIEFING ACTIVITIES THAT BUILD POWER

Although the debriefing is an opportunity to undertake powerful learning about teaching for the teacher and the coach, a number of activities can be undertaken by the coach after the debriefing that create support for the coaching enterprise.

If the coach is not based in the school, it is a good idea to stop in to say hello to the principal on the way out of the school. It is important that the principal see the visible presence of professional development in the school. On other visits the coach may have the opportunity to speak at greater length with the principal about the quality work being undertaken by teachers, the power that has come from coaching, and the effects on student achievement.

Reflecting on the Visit

The coach should also take a few minutes after the visit to reflect on what occurred during the school visit. He or she may identify common confusions among teachers being coached or parts of procedures that require clarification. These concerns can then be revisited in whole-group coaching sessions. The coach might also identify teachers whose work can lead to clarification or teachers who can provide an excellent example that can be shared with the whole group.

In her role as a university-level coach of coaches, Emily often accompanies coaches on school visits to observe them work with teachers and provide feedback afterward. She and her collaborators sometimes ask coaches to write reflections on these visits, with a focus on the interpersonal relationships with teachers. The following reflection by Lori captures her insights on many of the features of a school visit that we have discussed in this chapter, including the need for demonstration over talk:

> I need to first demonstrate and teach before I can prompt for it. . . .
> I need to keep reminding myself that [coaching] is very new and
> different for many of the teachers I am working with and will
> work with in the future. I need to be a good teacher to them also.
> So instead of asking them to verbalize in the abstract, I need to
> coach during school visits to model the appropriate action for the
> situation, if that would be the most effective, instead of waiting
> for the lesson to be over. This way the teacher will be able to see
> how the action affects the lesson. . . . At a school I visited Monday
> I coached for and modeled teaching during the first reading of
> the new book. The teacher was asking the child what the word
> was, which was not getting results. I asked her to have the child
> reread and think about the story. The child did so and the results
> were favorable. By seeing how prompting for strategies worked
> and allowing the child to problem-solve more independently, the
> lesson was much stronger for the teacher than by me just telling
> her what she should have done after the fact.

Arwa's reflection also offers insight on the rehearsal and feedback work of the coach:

> After modeling or role-playing with a teacher, it is important to allow the teacher an opportunity to practice the task. This will allow the teacher to apply the task to her teaching and time to ask questions of clarification, before working with a student. . . . It is important to let the teachers know what they are doing well by providing them with positive feedback after the visit. One reason, which Emily pointed out, was in case the teacher was doing it by accident, the positive feedback brings it to the teacher's awareness. When working with teachers in the future, I will be more aware of the level of support provided by the teacher during the new-book introduction and the first reading of a book. If the teacher gives too much support, the running record the next day may give a false sense of text-level difficulty.

Setting Goals for Coaching Work

While these written reflections provide useful insight into the work that coaches do as a part of their debriefing, Emily has also worked with a large number of coaches to identify goals that might result from collaborative analysis. These goals provide a useful summary for this chapter:

- Have the teacher summarize understandings gained and goals for teaching.
- Work more frequently with specific examples from the lesson and explore them in an in-depth way with the teacher. This creates a more collaborative session whereby the teacher and coach work together to understand where shifts in teaching can occur.
- Be less directive in telling the teacher what changes needed to occur. This may have been more appropriate early in the year when teachers were learning certain teaching procedures, but now this transmission model of debriefing needs to be faded out in favor of a more collaborative approach. There may still be room for telling, but this should not characterize the tone of the school visit.
- Have the teacher summarize understandings gained and goals for teaching.
- Work more frequently with students as part of the debriefing experience with the teacher. The power of this will be obvious

on the first school visit. Working with the student can provide a demonstration for the teacher or be a part of a genuine puzzling out and gathering of more information about the student's processing. It is an effective way to get a shift in a teacher's instructional practices.

CONCLUSION

We began this chapter by borrowing from Richardson (1996) to explain that the classroom visit is a unique opportunity to build a deep level of professional knowledge. Since professional knowledge is closely tied to action, by having the coach work to change the action of teachers, the coach is able to change professional practice. Although this work is difficult, the coach has a number of strategies and opportunities, which we have discussed in the preceding chapters, that might be employed. In the following chapter we discuss the implications of coaching as a form of professional development and the challenges and possibilities it poses.

CHAPTER 10

Literacy Coaching: Building the Capacity for Systemic Change

Interest in teacher professional development, particularly coaching, is at an all-time high (Lyons, 2007). In the past 5 years or so, millions of dollars in Reading First grants have been awarded to states to support literacy instruction, including coaching initiatives. Even more significant than this federally funded effort, states and districts have also worked at a more local level to fund coaching positions. As a result, thousands of literacy coaches are now working in schools to support teachers.

Because literacy coaching has gained such rapid popularity, educators are trying to catch up by making what we know about coaching more accessible. The International Reading Association and the National Council of Teachers of English have launched the Literacy Coaching Clearinghouse (http://www.literacycoachingonline.org), a new resource for educators who want to learn more about coaching. Further evidence of the interest in coaching comes from the fact that in just the past few years, at least 10 different organizations have published 13 different lists of characteristics of effective professional development (Guskey, 2003).

We conclude our volume on coaching with recommendations for administrators, researchers, teachers, and of course the coaches themselves. Our recommendations come from research and from our own case study work coaching literacy coaches. We link our recommendations to Guskey's (2003) three conclusions about professional development:

1. Student achievement is the ultimate criteria to evaluate the effectiveness of professional development initiatives.
2. We need clear descriptions of the settings of professional development initiatives because they are so contextually bound; what works in one setting might not work in another.

3. There are teachers who have found effective ways to help students learn. We need to identify these practices and share them.

RECOMMENDATIONS FOR ADMINISTRATORS

Fullan (1993) related an analysis by Pascale (1990), who explains that "when there is consensus above, and pressure below, things happen" (p. 126). The task for administrators, then, is to build consensus to meet school-level objectives; in other words, to create the need or desire for change. Without this agreement at the top about the need for change, the status quo is maintained.

As Fullan (1993) pointed out, however, pressure from below is also necessary for change to occur. By itself, consensus at the top about the need for change can lead to feelings of anxiety, especially on the part of teachers. The school board meeting would probably sound like this:

> FIRST SCHOOL BOARD MEMBER: Our third-grade tests are abysmal. They have gone down 7 years in a row. What do the principals have to say about this?
>
> SUPERINTENDENT: Yes, they know about it, and they are concerned too. We had a big meeting with all of our principals and district coordinators last week to review these scores. We have got to do something about this trend. Soon we'll be at the bottom of all the districts in the state. Should we bring in an outside evaluator to see what we're doing wrong?
>
> SECOND SCHOOL BOARD MEMBER: We brought in an outside evaluator 5 years ago, and she wrote a 50-page report saying that scores were low and that if things didn't change we would be in this kind of trouble.
>
> THIRD SCHOOL BOARD MEMBER: I talked to the third-grade teachers and they are really upset too. They really thought their scores would change this year.
>
> FOURTH SCHOOL BOARD MEMBER: Well, we all agree! Things have got to change!

The administrators in this fictional example are absolutely right because things do need to change. The school board members have also done a good job of building consensus, but consensus by itself will not bring about change, only hand-wringing. Pascale (1990) argued that, in addition to consensus from the top, pressure from the bottom is a second necessary ingredient.

The word *pressure* can have unpleasant connotations; we think Pascale used it to connote something positive: energy for change. A simple analogy comes from everyday life. An entire family might agree that a new sofa would look far better against the window, but unless someone places energy behind moving the sofa, the furniture arrangement will remain the same. In its simplest terms, for change to occur we need agreement that it needs to happen and then pressure, or energy, to make it happen.

We propose that administrators think of literacy coaching as providing the necessary pressure for change, as a tool for ongoing professional renewal that will lead to enhanced student learning. From this perspective, then, coaches become a necessary part of the school environment and not simply a temporary support brought in during academic emergencies.

Once districts have literacy coaches in place, an important caveat for administrators is to resist a one-size-fits-all approach because, as Guskey (2003) noted, professional development is very much contextually bound. What works in one school may not be what is needed in another school. Different objectives might be articulated for different schools, or the same objective might be proposed for a particular grade level across a district with the understanding that different schools may have different ways of achieving the goal. By recognizing the inventiveness of each school staff, administrators can tailor the deployment of coaches to support the achievement of educational goals.

A final recommendation for administrators is that literacy coaches be selected with great care; it is not sufficient for a coach to have a high degree of both knowledge and skills. The disposition of the literacy coach is also critical. For this reason districts should avoid hiring coaches on the basis of only years of service or previous administrative backgrounds. School districts that hire coaches who are not highly trained in content, who do not know how to teach that content, and/or who do not have the disposition to work with all stakeholders will only get simplistic approaches to coaching—approaches that may not be effective in changing teaching and affecting student learning.

In the long run administrators need to think about a long-term vision of literacy coaching. Despite the cost and difficulty of training and supporting coaches in establishing their coaching practice, we would suggest that coaching networks begin to think about how they can periodically rotate, perhaps on a 5- or 8-year interval, personnel through the coaching positions. We say this because we know coaching networks are vulnerable to staffing decisions.

By rotating coaches we build capacity and convey the message that the coaching network is not about a person, but about a professional vision for renewal. We also dilute the power held by a particular individual to allow accessibility to ownership by all participants. Guskey (2003) explained that different teachers find different ways of being effective in supporting student learning, and the same is true of coaches, so returning experienced coaches full time to the classroom means their teaching expertise can be fully focused on children. Indeed the rotation of personnel through the coaching position is just one aspect of developing renewal for what we hope will eventually become vintage coaching sites.

RECOMMENDATIONS FOR RESEARCHERS

Obviously there is much work to be undertaken by researchers on literacy coaching, and a number of individuals and teams have already started that work. On the individual level, L'Allier (2005) initiated a small-scale but exceedingly labor-intensive enterprise featuring a few schools, a small group of coaches, and one university faculty member.

At the citywide level Fisher, Lapp, Frey, and Flood (2006) provided a very powerful example of how San Diego City Schools, San Diego State University, and the teachers' association worked together to articulate procedures for how coaches and teachers can work together.

Rita Bean (2001, 2004a, 2004b) has been active for a number of years on the statewide level; while on the national and international levels Lyons, Pinnell, and DeFord (1993) articulated the role of the reading coach in the very specific context of Reading Recovery, a short-term literacy intervention for first-grade students.

What is significant about this range of work is that it offers researchers a number of possibilities for how research may be approached. We suggest here three lines of inquiry related to literacy coaching that emerge as a result of our review of the literature:

1. Developing valid and meaningful ways to measure the impact of coaching.
2. Describing how effective coaches coach.
3. Examining the short- and long-term benefits of coaching.

We discuss each of these lines of inquiry in the sections that follow.

Measuring the Impact of Coaching

We happened to take a break while writing this section to get some takeout food for dinner. We always enjoy reading the messages in our fortune cookies, but this time, Adrian's seemed particularly apropos. It said: "A difference, to be a difference, must make a difference."

We could not agree more. To decide whether coaching has made a difference, we need to look for fundamental changes; for us that means coaching matters if it makes a difference to student achievement. It is wonderful if coaching changes teacher attitudes, beliefs, and even teaching practices, but unless student achievement changes, coaching has really not made a difference.

This task is not a straightforward one. Linking student change to coaching will not be easy. Even when we try to focus on student outcomes as a measure of impact, we sometimes lapse into reporting teacher perceptions of change instead. It is not sufficient to use teacher self-reports about student change as a measure of student improvement. Instead, as Guskey noted (2003), we need to push beyond measuring impact and effectiveness by using teacher reports and move toward examining improvement in student outcomes (see for example, Rodgers, Fullerton, & Deford, 2001).

How we measure student outcomes in relation to coaching will be a task for future study. Consumers of research should expect and demand high-quality research in this regard and not settle for weak assertions of links between coaching and student achievement.

Describing How Effective Coaches Coach

By building research agendas that examine the link between coaching and student outcomes, researchers will be able to address a number of new questions, such as, How do effective coaches coach?

This inquiry directed at the work of coaches will likely begin with the questions, What do coaches do when they observe teaching? and How do they make decisions about the quality of that teaching? Such work may lead to more detailed specifications of what works for coaching in different settings. The next component of such research involves how coaches coach (see the work on developing rubrics reported in Chapter 4 of this volume; this work is being led by researchers David Kerbow, Anthony Bryk, Gay Pinnell, Pat Scharer, and Irene Fountas). It also involves examining how teachers change teaching practices to better support student learning. The essential focus here is understanding and describing how coaching makes a difference.

Examining the Short- and Long-Term Benefits of Coaching

Finally, a third line of inquiry might involve the short- and long-term gains of coaching and whether the costs of implementing coaching as a part of professional development are justified. Even here we must be cautious. For example, if literacy coaching is limited to first grade and students cannot maintain gains in second grade, analysts should not assume that coaching does not work.

Instead, other questions need to be posed, such as Why could the students' gains from first grade not be maintained into second grade? Perhaps the coaching needs to be extended to second grade. The answers are likely to be robust as we begin to identify the various ways in which teachers are able to help individual students.

RECOMMENDATIONS FOR TEACHERS

One seemingly intractable issue that we encounter in coaching is the challenge to teachers of making the private public. Wilson and Daviss (1994) explained:

> Rarely, if ever, do most practicing U.S. teachers come together to study each other's work and help each other to become better teachers. Schools as institutions and education as a profession effectively allow teachers no continuing opportunities systematically to improve their own effectiveness in the classroom. (p. 88)

Wilson and Daviss went on to declare that "teachers normally meet regularly at only three places: the faculty lounge, faculty meetings, and union meetings [and that] other traditions and taboos of the teaching profession inhibit teachers from sharing innovations" (p. 88). Barth (in Wilson and Daviss, 1994) elaborated on these taboos, suggesting that because of the "deep respect for the profession's ethic of individualism—and, therefore, for each teacher's autonomy in her own classroom. 'A taboo prevents one teacher from watching another . . . engaged in the act of teaching'" (p. 91). Barth explained that "unless adults talk with one another, observe one another, and help one another, very little will change. There can be no community of learners when there is no community and when there are no learners" (p. 91).

What these three theorists pose for teachers is the challenge to work more collaboratively with the goal of reflecting and acting on teaching. We would go one step further and suggest that if schools do not support opportunities for teachers to collaborate, they must seek these opportunities for themselves. We propose that by working as a group, teachers can create their own communities; and with the assistance of a qualified coach, this community can become even more powerful and robust.

Several years ago, when we were both teachers and members of the Newfoundland and Labrador Teachers' Association, we were able to take part in a program called T4: Teachers Talking to Teachers. Our professional association funded very small grants that permitted release time or local travel so that teachers with similar interests could visit each other and talk. Our participation had a powerful impact on us, perhaps because the success of the program lay in its ability to capitalize on the social nature of our profession.

Although it may be that we practice our teaching in private, we love to talk about it with other professionals when given the opportunity, and we love the primacy of personal contact as a way of talking about it. We contend that although the structure of schools forces isolation, when teachers are given the opportunity to talk, they will do so and at length. Isolation is not the issue at all. Actually the problem is the structuring of time to meet and the identification of a qualified coach to offer teachers support that fosters deep inquiry.

These are problems for literacy coaching that can be solved with adequate supports. Guskey (2003) proposed that different teachers have found different effective ways for different students to learn, and by observing one another they can learn of these techniques on a firsthand basis.

We acknowledge that making our teaching public comes with considerable risk, so being a teacher in a coaching network will require a willingness to reflect on and act on teaching in group settings. Teachers who wish to participate will need to collaborate, take risks, and accept commentary and observations from others.

With this risk comes the opportunity to tie both one's own and other teachers' knowledge and experience with the recommendations of a coach to yield the robust results possible in a coaching setting. Through seeking understanding rather than answers and by posing many questions, the link between teaching and learning can become even clearer.

RECOMMENDATIONS FOR COACHES

Although there are many tasks that can be undertaken by administrators, researchers, and teachers that will support literacy coaching, clearly the literacy coach is the single individual most responsible for supporting teachers in developing their teaching within the coaching context. The coach has the difficult job of understanding the multiple missions that may have been identified by administrators, of working with researchers who may also be stakeholders in the coaching enterprise, and of working with many teachers who may face a range of challenges. For this reason, we have divided our recommendations to coaches into the following four parts.

Providing Instructional Leadership

A few years back, a trend that swept through the principalship was the concept of the principal as the school's instructional leader. While the concept is a powerful one, it is fraught with difficulty.

Because the principal often acts in a supervisory capacity over teachers and conducts summative evaluations of them, it is difficult for the principal to lead instruction as a partner with teachers. Additionally, the principal often has content area preparation unique to a particular discipline, and so leadership ability in the out-of-content area is limited. While the concept of leadership in instruction may be useful for conceptualizing the principalship, the ability to lead in a hands-on way is difficult. The coach, however, can support teachers by acting as an instructional leader and by supporting teachers who can also take leadership roles.

While the coach must work closely with the principal to both understand the mission of the school and the objectives of professional development (as well as facilitate the time and space demanded by coaching), the coach must work in a way so that he or she is not seen as an extension of building-level administration.

Since coaches must work to gain the trust of teachers, if they are viewed as administrators, teachers will understandably remain guarded, making working at the edge of teachers' knowledge impossible. It is essential that the coach-teacher relationship be a forthright one if the participants are to fully understand the nuances of the teaching context that Guskey (2003) tells us is essential.

Building Ownership

Working with administrators is not the only relationship that literacy coaches need to cultivate. Indeed, since coaches work with a variety of constituents, from principals and teachers to researchers, school board members, and parents, it is essential that the coach work to build ownership by all the participants. Part of this work is leading participants in the resolution of problems using negotiation. It is necessary that the stakeholders negotiate with each other as well as within their own ranks, and the coach acts to both facilitate and mediate this work.

One of the difficulties of building ownership is negotiating the degree to which participants are directed by the coach or supported by the coach. We call this problem the *constructivist-transmission paradox*. For instance, even though we purport to take a constructivist stance regarding coaching throughout this book, vestiges of the transmission model of teaching and learning remain. Some of our colleagues have suggested that it is presumptuous to tell a teacher how to teach. We disagree.

We argue that unlike faculty, coaches are (or should be) insiders at schools. In a coaching context, the coach will sometimes have an answer that the teacher may not. Sometimes the teacher will have the answer, and, of course, at other times both coach and teacher will find answers together. To us this is not a transmission model. Additionally, when we do use the word *answer,* we don't mean a recipe, but rather the next iteration of the professional development initiative. This is all to be expected if indeed teachers and coaches take turns being the expert in their interactions, and it is a sign of building ownership. It is this ownership by all participants that is essential to ensure that all educators have a stake in student learning.

Developing Vision

Given the lack of supports such as extensive funding, large numbers of consultants, and large-scale data gathering and analysis that can be supplied from top-down initiatives, it is up to coaches to build their own infrastructure to support coaching efforts. One important feature of establishing a coaching effort is determining the procedures that participants and stakeholders will follow in the network. Since the goal is to instantiate coaching into the structure and culture of schools, coaches need to understand that they will likely live with the decisions they make for a very long time.

Therefore coaches establishing a coaching effort must think carefully about their decisions so they do not give up essential elements that could contribute to success. They must also agree to periodically renegotiate their relationship with other participants so that necessary changes can be realized. Stating these essentials at the beginning of the relationship will set the framework for subsequent negotiations and help navigate the twists and turns of each context.

Building Coaching Capacity

The coaching conversations that occur between the literacy coach and a teacher or group of teachers represent the most powerful opportunity to share insight into teaching and learning. In part this is because in conversations the coach and teachers can problem-solve around tricky parts of teaching (Pinnell & Rodgers, 2002). As a literacy coach develops coaching capacity, it is important that he or she work toward early successful experiences in problem solving. By doing so, coaches can develop powerful allies in teachers and have an effect on student learning.

Another role of the coach that engenders high receptivity among teachers is teachers' ability to structure learning from each other. While it may be alien to teachers to observe one another, teachers are very interested in learning the latest so-called tricks. The added power in the literacy coaching position is that the coach, using "self analysis and self reflection" (Pinnell & Rodgers, 2002, p. 189), can transfer these tricks into deep-level learning by helping teachers in "thinking our way forward" (p. 189). What is most important about the coach-teacher conversation and the teacher-teacher observation is that both provide a venue for coaching that is grounded in real teaching of children and not book study.

While it is inspiring to think that teachers can work together as a part of a ground-up initiative, we are not kidding ourselves here. We know of and have worked with teachers in coaching settings who were hostile, sat stone-faced through a coaching session, and refused to participate in the reflection and debriefing afterward.

As we try to build coaching capacity, we might wonder who would want to work with those teachers and subject themselves to such treatment. Indeed, when discussing the dispositions of some teachers in coaching networks, we have heard teachers use language like "well poisoners" and "snipers" to describe their colleagues. These attitudes are especially apparent during conversations between teachers and their coach.

We think that prior to the establishment of coaching networks, all participants should acknowledge that the willingness to be coached requires a certain disposition of teachers. Some excellent teachers may not have this disposition, and so it is essential that careful thought be given to teachers' dispositions in the development of fledgling networks. By taking time to identify teachers who will respond well in a coaching setting, a focus on student achievement through a study of teacher practices can be undertaken.

CONCLUSION

Coaches are multipurposed school-based staff developers who tailor their activities around the needs of particular teachers and groups of teachers. Their work is contextualized around the state of practice in a school and around the level of expertise of teachers. There are many ways to define coaching. Some may think of it as an administrative task, but for us observations and conversations are a critical part of coaching.

Because the current interest in coaching represents a new wave in thinking about how we teach, teachers play a critical role. In this book we have proposed that coaching is a dialogue in which teachers, coaches, and instructional leaders all participate. We all need to know how to do it— what our roles are and how to carry them out—so that we can all do the coaching of each other. Because it's no straightforward matter to coach, teachers themselves must coach the coach on how to optimize support. The teacher being coached has a key role to play in shaping the coaching process and cannot be ignored.

If we can change the way we teach, we can reach in an even more powerful way the children we were already reaching; we can even reach children who did not respond to our teaching previously. As Adrian and a colleague wrote in a recent article:

> Because bottom-up change puts a lot of freight on the individuals involved, revisioning past practices using collaborative reform is difficult to begin, difficult to sustain, and risky for the participants to complete whilst still sustaining the consensus of the group. Utmost caution is essential. Nevertheless, there are many rewards to be unearthed in the conversations between the different stakeholders that provide the opportunity for traditional . . . [ways of working] to become renewed through collaborative professional efforts. (Rodgers & Keil, 2007)

Not everyone will want to take part in such a high-risk effort. Therefore it is essential that we learn from our mistakes as we capitalize on our successes to instantiate coaching capacity into an otherwise resistant school structure and culture. We must ride the crest of the trend that is coaching and rapidly work toward researching our efforts to avoid exhausting what some too easily could come to consider a fad.

References

Bean, J. C. (2001). *Engaging ideas: The professor's guide to integrating writing, critical thinking, and active learning in the classroom.* San Francisco: Jossey-Bass.

Bean, R. (2004a). *The reading specialist: Leadership for the classroom, school, and community.* New York: Guilford Press.

Bean, R. (2004b, December). *Becoming a literacy coach: The first year in Reading First schools.* Paper presented at the annual meeting of the National Reading Conference, San Antonio, TX.

Block, C. C., Oaker, M., & Hurt, N. (2002). The expertise of literacy teachers: A continuum from preschool to grade 5. *Reading Research Quarterly, 37,* 178–206.

Bloom, B. S., & Krathwohl, D. R. (1965). *The taxonomy of educational objectives, the classification of educational goals. Handbook I: Cognitive domain.* New York: D. McKay.

Bloom, D., & Egan-Robertson, A. (1993). The social construction of intertextuality in classroom reading and writing lessons. *Reading Research Quarterly, 28,* 305–333.

Cazden, C. (1983). Adult assistance to language development: Scaffolds, models and direct instruction. In R. P. Parker (Ed.), *Developing literacy: Young children's use of language* (pp. 3–18). Newark, DE: International Reading Association.

Cazden, C. (1986). Classroom discourse. In M. C. Wittrock (Ed.), *Handbook of research of teaching* (pp. 432–463). New York: Longman.

Clay, M. M. (1991). *Becoming literate: The construction of inner control.* Portsmouth, NH: Heinemann.

Clay, M. M. (1993). *Reading Recovery: A guidebook for teachers in training.* Portsmouth, NH: Heinemann.

Clay, M. M. (1998). *By different paths to common outcomes.* York, ME: Stenhouse.

Clay, M. M. (2000). *Running records for classroom teachers.* Auckland, New Zealand: Heinemann.

Clay, M. M. (2001). *Change over time in children's literacy achievement.* Portsmouth, NH: Heinemann.

Clay, M. M. (2002). *An observation survey of early literacy achievement* (2nd ed.). Portsmouth, NH: Heinemann.

Cohen, D. K. (1990). A revolution in one classroom: The case of Mrs. Oublier. *Education Evaluation and Policy Analysis, 12,* 311–329.

Cruickshank, D. R. (1985). *Models for the preparation of America's teachers.* Bloomington, IN: Phi Delta Kappa.

Darling-Hammond, L. (1996). What matters most: A competent teacher for every child. *Phi Delta Kappan, 78,* 193–200.

Dewey, J. (1944). *Democracy and education.* New York: Macmillan.

Dewey, J. (1960). *How we think.* Lexington, MA: D. C. Heath.

Dirkx, J. M. (2001). The power of feelings: Emotion, imagination, and the construction of meaning in adult learning. *New Directions for Adult and Continuing Education, 89,* 63–72.

Dole, J. A. (2004). The changing role of the reading specialist in school reform. *The Reading Teacher, 57*(5), 462–471.

Evertson, C. M., & Green, J. L. (1986). Observation as inquiry and method. In M. C. Wittrock (Ed.), *Handbook of research on teaching* (3rd ed., pp. 162–213). New York: Macmillan.

Ferro, T. R. (1993). The influence of affective processing in education and training. *New Directions for Adult and Continuing Education, 59,* 22–33.

Fisher, D., Lapp, D., Frey, N., & Flood, J. (2006). *Selecting the peer coach: Lessons from a large urban district.* Paper presented at the annual meeting of the National Reading Conference, Miami, FL.

Freire, P. (1993). *Pedagogy of the oppressed* (2nd ed.). New York: Continuum.

Fullan, M. G. (1991). *The new meaning of educational change* (2nd ed.). New York: Teachers College Press.

Fullan, M. (1993). *Change forces: Probing the depth of educational reform.* New York: Falmer Press.

Fullan, M., & Hargreaves, A. (1996). *What's worth fighting for in your school?* New York: Teachers College Press.

Giebelhaus, C. R. (1994). The mechanical third ear device: A student teaching supervision alternative. *Journal of Teacher Education, 45,* 365–373.

Grimmett, P. P., Moody, P. R., & Balasubramaniam, M. (1985, April). *District-wide implementation of peer coaching: A case study of one step toward successful change.* Paper presented at the annual meeting of the American Educational Research Association, San Francisco.

Guskey, T. R. (2003). What makes professional development effective? *Phi Delta Kappa, 84,* 748–750.

Halliday, M. A. K. (1975). *Learning how to mean: Explorations in the development of language.* London, UK: Edward Arnold.

Hobsbaum, A., Peters, S., & Sylva, K. (1996). Scaffolding in Reading Recovery. *Oxford Review of Education, 22*(1), 17–35.

Hops, H., Davis, B., & Longoria, N. (1995). Methodological issues in direct observation: Illustrations with the Living in Familial Environments (LIFE) coding system. *Journal of Clinical Child Psychology, 24,* 193–203.

Hughes, M. T., Cash, M. M., Ahwee, S., & Klingner, J. (2002). A national overview of professional development programs in reading. In E. Rodgers & G. S. Pinnell (Eds.), *Learning from teaching in literacy education: New perspectives on professional development* (pp. 9–28). Portsmouth, NH: Heinemann.

International Reading Association. (2004). *The role and qualifications of the reading coach in the United States*. Newark, DE: Author.

International Reading Association. (December 2005–January 2006). IRA, NCTE form literacy coaches clearinghouse. *Reading Today, 23*(3), 3.

Joyce, B., & Showers, B. (1988). *Staff achievement through staff development: Fundamentals of school renewal* (2nd ed.). White Plains, NY: Longman.

Joyce, B., & Showers, B. (1995). *Student achievement through staff development*. White Plains, NY: Longman.

Kinnucan-Welsch, K., Rosemary, C. A., & Grogan, P. R. (2006). Accountability by design in literacy professional development. *The Reading Teacher, 59*(5), 426–435.

L'Allier, S. K. (2005, December). *Mentoring literacy coaches: Facilitating the development of knowledge, observation tools, and effective coaching techniques*. Paper presented at the annual meeting of the National Reading Conference, Miami, FL.

Lambert, L., Walker, D., Zimmerman, D., Cooper, J. E., Lambert, M., Gardner, M., & Slack, P. (1995). *The constructivist leader*. New York: Teachers College Press.

Lewis, C., Perry, R., & Murata, A. (2006, April). How should research contribute to instructional improvement? The case of lesson study. *Educational Researcher, 35*(3), 3–14.

Lindfors, J. W. (1999). *Children's inquiry: Using language to make sense of the world*. New York: Teachers College Press.

Luria, A. (1979). *The making of mind*. Cambridge, MA: Harvard University Press.

Luria, A. R. (1982). *Language and cognition*. New York: Wiley.

Lyons, C. A. (1993). The use of questions in the teaching of high-risk beginning readers: A profile of a developing Reading Recovery teacher. *Reading and Writing Quarterly: Overcoming Learning Difficulties, 9*(4), 317–327.

Lyons, C. A. (1994). Constructing chains of reasoning in Reading Recovery demonstration lessons. In D. Leu & C. Kinzer (Eds.), *Multidimensional aspects of literacy research, theory and practice. Forty-third yearbook of the National Reading Conference* (pp. 276–286). Chicago: National Reading Conference.

Lyons, C. A. (1999). Emotions, cognition, and becoming a reader: A message to teachers of struggling learners. *Literacy Teaching and Learning, 4*(1), 67–87.

Lyons, C. A. (2002). Becoming an effective literacy coach: What does it take? In E. M. Rodgers & G. S. Pinnell (Eds.), *Learning from teaching in literacy education: New perspectives on professional development* (pp. 93–118). Portsmouth, NH: Heinemann.

Lyons, C. A. (2003). *Teaching struggling readers: How to use brain-based research to maximize learning*. Portsmouth, NH: Heinemann.

Lyons, C. A. (2007, February). *Becoming an effective coach*. Paper presented at the Southeastern Regional Reading Recovery and Early Literacy Conference, Savannah, GA.

Lyons, C. A., & Pinnell, G. S. (2001). *Systems for change in literacy education: A guide to professional development*. Portsmouth, NH: Heinemann.

Lyons, C., Pinnell, G. S., & DeFord, D. (1993). *Partners in learning: Teachers and children in Reading Recovery*. New York: Teachers College Press.

Maloch, B. (2002). Scaffolding student talk: One teacher's role in literature discussion groups. *Reading Research Quarterly, 37*(1), 94–112.

Many, J. (2002). An exhibition and analyses of verbal tapestries: Understanding how scaffolding is woven into the fabric of instructional conversations. *Reading Research Quarterly, 37*, 376–407.

Morgan, N., & Saxton, J. (1994). *Asking better questions: Models, techniques, and classroom activities for engaging students in learning*. Markham, Ontario: Pembroke.

National Council of Teachers of English. (2004, November). Taking a look at literacy coaching. *The Council Chronicle, 14*(2), 1.

Pascale, P. (1990). *Managing on the edge*. New York: Touchstone.

Patton, M. Q. (1990). *Qualitative evaluation and research methods*. New York: Sage.

Phillips, M. D., & Glickman, C. D. (1991). Peer coaching: Developmental approach to enhancing teacher thinking. *Journal of Staff Development, 12*(2), 21–25.

Pinnell, G. S., & Rodgers, E. M. (2002). Making decisions as professional developers. In E. Rodgers & G. S. Pinnell (Eds.), *Learning from teaching in literacy education: New perspectives on professional development* (pp. 173–190). Portsmouth, NH: Heinemann.

Poglinco, S. M., Bach, A. J., Hovde, K., Rosenblum, S., Saunders, M., & Supovitz, J. A. (2003). *The heart of the matter: The coaching model in America's choice schools*. Philadelphia: Consortium for Policy and Research in Education.

Richardson, V. (1996). The role of attitudes and beliefs in learning to teach. In J. Sikula (Ed.), *Handbook of research on teacher education* (2nd ed., pp. 102–119). New York: Simon & Schuster, Macmillan.

Rodgers, A. (2002). Old roads and new paths: What happens when two teachers attempt an alternative teaching strategy within a peer collaborative relationship. In E. Rodgers & G. S. Pinnell (Eds.), *Learning from teaching in literacy education: New perspectives on professional development* (pp. 135–157). Portsmouth, NH: Heinemann.

Rodgers, A., & Keil, V. (2007). Restructuring a traditional student teacher supervision model: Fostering enhanced professional development and mentoring within a professional development school context. *Teaching and Teacher Education, 32*(1), 63–80.

Rodgers, A., & Rodgers, E. (Eds.). (2004). *Scaffolding literacy instruction: Strategies for K–4 classrooms*. Portsmouth, NH: Heinemann.

Rodgers, A., & Rodgers, E. (2006). Preparing for diversity: Professional development for today's teachers. In B. Honchell & M. Schulz (Eds.), *Literacy for diverse learners* (pp. 262–294). Norwood, MA: Christopher-Gordon.

Rodgers, E. (2000a). Collaborative inquiry in Reading Recovery, or "Why sit in a circle?" *The Running Record, 13*(2), 6–7.

Rodgers, E. (2000b). When is a scaffold really a scaffold? In T. Shanahan & F. Rodriguez-Brown (Eds.), *Forty-ninth yearbook of the National Reading Conference* (pp. 78–90). Chicago: National Reading Conference.

Rodgers, E. (2004). Interactions that scaffold reading performance. *Journal of Literacy Research, 36,* 501–532.

Rodgers, E., Fullerton, S., & DeFord, D. (2001). What does it take to reform instructional practices? In J. V. Hoffman, D. L. Schallert, C. M. Fairbands, J. Worthy, & B. Maloch (Eds.), *Fiftieth yearbook of the National Reading Conference* (pp. 519–531). Chicago: National Reading Conference.

Rodgers, E., & Pinnell, G. S. (Eds.). (2002). *Learning from teaching in literacy education: New perspectives on professional development.* Portsmouth, NH: Heinemann.

Rodgers, E., & Rodgers, A. (2004). The role of scaffolding in teaching. In A. Rodgers & E. Rodgers (Eds.), *Strategies for scaffolding literacy instruction in K–4 classrooms* (pp. 1–10). Portsmouth, NH: Heinemann.

Rogoff, B. (1990). *Apprenticeship in thinking: Cognitive development in social context.* New York: Oxford University Press.

Rogoff, B. (1997). Observing sociocultural activity on three planes: Participatory appropriation, guided participation, and apprenticeship. In J. V. Wertsch, P. Del Rio, & A. Alverez (Eds.), *Sociocultural studies of mind* (pp. 139–164). New York: Cambridge University Press.

Rosenblatt, L. (2002, December). *A pragmatist theoretician looks at research: Implications and questions calling for answers.* Paper presented at the annual meeting of the National Reading Conference, Miami, FL.

Sarason, S. (1990). *The predictable failure of educational reform.* San Francisco: Jossey-Bass.

Schön, D. (1983). *The reflective practitioner: How professionals think in action.* New York: Basic Books.

Shaw, M. L., Smith, W. E., Chesler, B. J., & Romeo, L. (2005, June/July). Moving forward: The reading specialist as literacy coach. *Reading Today, 22,* 10–11.

Shulman, L. S. (1986, February). Knowledge and teaching: Foundations of the new reform. *Harvard Educational Review, 57*(1), 1–22.

Sprinthall, N. A., Reiman, A. J., & Theis-Sprinthall, L. (1996). Teacher professional development. In J. Sikula (Ed.), *Handbook of research on teacher education* (2nd ed., pp. 666–703). New York: Simon & Schuster, Macmillan.

Strauss, A., & Corbin, J. (1998). *Basics of qualitative research.* Thousand Oaks, CA: Sage.

Strickland, D. (2004, April). *Developing strategies for improving reading achievement through professional development.* Paper presented at the annual meeting of the American Educational Research Association, San Diego, CA.

Tharp, R. G., & Gallimore, R. (1988). *Rousing minds to life: Teaching, learning, and schooling in social context.* New York: Cambridge University Press.

Toll, C. (2004). *The literacy coach's survival guide: Essential questions and practical answers*. Newark, DE: International Reading Association.

Toll, C. (2005, December). *Models of literacy coaching and their political implications*. Paper presented at the annual meeting of the National Reading Conference, Miami, FL.

Vygotsky, L. S. (1978). *Mind in society: The development of higher psychological processes*. Cambridge, MA: Harvard University Press.

Walpole, S., & McKenna, M. C. (2004). *The literacy coach's handbook: A guide to research-based practice*. New York: Guilford.

Wang, J., & Odell, J. S. (2002). Mentored learning to teach according to standards-based reform: A critical review. *Review of Educational Research, 72*(3), 481–546.

Wells, G. (1999). *Dialogic inquiry: Towards a sociocultural practice and theory of education*. New York: Cambridge University Press.

Wells, G. (2000). Vygotskian perspectives on literacy research: Constructing meaning through collaborative inquiry. In C. D. Lee & P. Smagorinsky (Eds.), *Dialogic inquiry in education* (pp. 51–85). New York: Cambridge University Press.

Wilson, K. G., & Daviss, B. (1994). *Redesigning education*. New York: Henry Holt.

Wong, S., Groth, L., O'Flahavan, J., Gale, S., Kelley, G., Leeds, S., Regetz, J., & O'Malley-Steiner, J. (1994). *Characterizing teacher-student interaction in Reading Recovery lessons* (Reading Research Report No. 17). Athens, GA: National Reading Research Center. (ERIC Document Reproduction Service No. ED 375 392).

Wood, D. (2003). The why, what, when, and how of tutoring: The development of helping and tutoring skills in children. *Literacy Teaching and Learning, 7*(1&2), 1–30.

Wood, D., Bruner, J., & Ross, G. (1976). The role of tutoring in problem-solving. *Journal of Child Psychology, 17*, 89–100.

Wood, D., & Middleton, D. (1975). A study of assisted problem-solving. *British Journal of Psychology, 66*(2), 181–191.

Wood, D., & Wood, H. (1996). Vygotsky, tutoring and learning. *Oxford Review of Education, 22*(1), 5–16.

Wren, S. (2005, December). *Literacy coaches: What research says and does not say*. Paper presented at the annual meeting of the National Reading Conference, Miami, FL.

Zeichner, K. M., & Liston, D. P. (1996). *Reflective teaching: An introduction*. Mahwah, NJ: Lawrence Erlbaum.

Index

About the Authors

Adrian Rodgers is an assistant professor in the School of Teaching and Learning at The Ohio State University in Newark, Ohio. He teaches methods courses in the preservice teacher education program. His research interests include literacy and professional development.

Emily M. Rodgers is an associate professor in the College of Education at The Ohio State University. Before joining Ohio State, Emily was a teacher for 10 years in Newfoundland. Her research has focused on the professional development of teachers and the nature of effective scaffolding of literacy learning. Her paper "Language Matters: When Is a Scaffold Really a Scaffold?" won the National Reading Conference's Outstanding Student Research Award in 1999.